WE'VE GOT
BLOG

WE'VE GOT
BLOG

HOW WEBLOGS ARE
CHANGING OUR CULTURE

From the Editors of Perseus Publishing

PERSEUS
PUBLISHING

Copyright © 2002 by Perseus Publishing
This collection was compiled and edited by John Rodzvilla.

Library of Congress Control Number: 2002104495
ISBN 0–7382–0741–1

Perseus Publishing is a member of the Perseus Books Group.
Find us on the World Wide Web at http://www.perseuspublishing.com

Perseus Publishing books are available at special discounts for bulk purchases in the U.S. by corporations, institutions, and other organizations. For more information, please contact the Special Markets Department at the Perseus Books Group, 11 Cambridge Center, Cambridge, MA 02142, or call (800) 255–1514 or (617) 252–5298, or e-mail j.mccrary@perseusbooks.com.
Text design by Brent Wilcox
Set in 11-point ITC Berkeley Book by the Perseus Books Group

First printing, June 2002
1 2 3 4 5 6 7 8 9 10—05 04 03 02

Contents

Introduction

THERE ARE ONLY A FEW THINGS YOU NEED TO KNOW ABOUT WEBLOGS.
First, of course, what are they?

A weblog is defined, these days, by its format: a frequently updated webpage with dated entries, new ones placed on top—but
that won't tell you everything you need to know.

The progenitors of the weblog movement adopted this format
as a matter of convenience, so that visitors could instantly see
their latest update, and whether it had been made a week, a day,
or an hour ago. But what drew them together, when they found
each other, was not their shared format: it was their love of the
World Wide Web, and the desire to share the things they found.

"Links with commentary, updated frequently" was the formula.
Experts at navigating the Web, the creators of these sites were in-
defatigable surfers, skilled searchers, and—as one early news
piece put it—relentless communicators. Their weblogs were
smart, irreverent, and reliably interesting, filters of a Web that
could no longer be completely catalogued.

When software developers set out to create tools to help people manage weblogs, it was natural that they would focus on the
sites' format rather than their function. It is a very literal way of
looking at a weblog, but from a programmer's point of view it de-
fines the problem to be solved. It is natural, too, that tools designed to accommodate the format changed the formula.

Since the earliest weblogs had required at least a rudimentary level of coding skill, the people who made them tended to be computer programmers and Web designers. All of them could be described as "power users" when it came to the Web, and for them, the Web was inherently interesting. But for those who required a tool to update their weblog, this was not always the case. Once literally *anyone* could make a weblog, literally anyone did.

The new webloggers, instead of focusing on the Web itself, used the Web to create social alliances and to broadcast tidbits of their days to those who were interested in reading them. People from all backgrounds and with all levels of technical skill began making weblogs; for them, the Web was a medium, not a passion.

Despite what you may have heard, the power of the weblog is in its form, not in the tool used to create it. But many of the people now making weblogs would be unable to exploit the form if it weren't for the tools that are now available.

Just as email has made us all writers, weblogs have made all of us publishers. And weblogs are publications, designed to be read by someone, whether it be a large global audience or (as is more commonly the case) a micro-audience of hundreds—or only a handful—of people.

So this is another thing you need to know: weblogs bring the Web—in theory a leveler, a democratic medium—to the People. To anyone with an Internet connection, the Web is now a two-way medium.

Weblogs are filtering the news, detailing daily lives, and providing editorial responses to the events of the day. For many people, a weblog is a soapbox from which they can proclaim their views, potentially influencing many more people than they can in their everyday lives. For others, a weblog is a creative space that allows them to experiment with the tools of the Web itself, or to document their offline projects for anyone who is interested. Some webloggers use their weblogs to tell personal stories, others to keep in touch with faraway friends and family. Businesses use weblogs to communicate with employees, and freelancers use them to build their reputations.

There is another thing to know about weblogs: they are native to the Web.

Unlike almost everything else online, weblogs are not just a digital variation on an established formula. Everything about them—their format, their reliance on links, their immediacy, their connections to each other—is derived from the medium in which they were born. They are of the Web itself.

Weblogs (and the community that has formed around them) run on links. Whether an individual weblog is focused on filtering the Web or filtering a single life, you probably will arrive there by following a link from another site, and when you get there, you will most likely find links to others. In the world of weblogs, traffic is currency. Almost all weblogs are non-commercial ventures: they don't make money for their maintainers, and in fact probably even cost them a little. Links—to and from other sites—are the coin of the realm.

The Web invented weblogs, but they are still being defined by the people who make them.

As the genre has matured, weblogs have gone in unexpected directions. There are photo weblogs, food weblogs, short-form diary weblogs, subject-specific weblogs, and one weblog that purports to be written by Julius Caesar—and which ran pop-up ads in support of several candidates during elections to the Roman senate in its imaginary world.

And why would anyone read them? Because they are fascinating.

Read any weblog for a few weeks and it is impossible not to feel that you know its writer. The best weblogs are those that convey the strongest personality. Every weblog has a point of view, and even those that contain no personal information reveal, over time, detailed maps of their creators' minds. It is captivating to see the biases, interests, and judgments of an individual reveal themselves so clearly.

If you are lucky, there is a weblog specific to your profession, providing you with one stop to keep abreast of industry news. Many webloggers comb through news sites, bringing to their readers' attention items they may have missed. Others use news articles only as a springboard for their own running commentary on the events of the day. If you are politically inclined, there are hundreds of weblogs maintained by individuals who are as passionate as you are about the left or the right.

Weblogs are the place for daily stories, impassioned reactions, mundane details, and miscellanea. They are as varied as their maintainers, and they are creating a generation of involved, impassioned citizens, and articulate, observant human beings.

They are a training ground for writers—and there is fine writing being produced daily on hundreds of sites. They are platforms for intelligent reaction to current events and ubiquitous pundits. They are repositories of Web trivia. They are desktop broadcasting. They are, as one early weblogger put it, pirate radio for the Web.

The articles in this collection are early reflections on the weblog phenomenon. Mature reflections do not exist: the weblog community coalesced only three years ago. Not even the pioneers—some of whom contributed to this anthology—know where weblogs are going, or what place they will eventually fill on the World Wide Web.

Most of the articles collected here appeared as real-time responses to the formation and expansion of the community as participants and observers attempted to make sense of the phenomenon that was growing around them. Like the weblogs that inspired them, they are thoughtful, brash, measured, pointed, enthusiastic, polished, and blunt. I hope reading them will inspire you to log on to the Web and investigate this new and growing genre—and maybe to create one of your own.

Rebecca Blood
February 2002

PART ONE
A Brief History

What the Hell
Is a Weblog and Why
Won't They Leave Me Alone?

A personal opinion by Derek M. Powazek
February 17, 2000

I FELL IN LOVE WITH THE WEB A LONG TIME AGO. IT ENTERED MY bloodstream like a virus, took root, and changed my life forever. And, almost immediately, the virus had to spread.

I made piles of homepages, the oldest of which are lost in the digital ether forever. I did my college thesis online. I got a job in the biz. I started lofty projects with vague goals like "doing it right." I cared too much.

And through it all, I drew my inspiration from the cacophony of personal voices I found online. Here was the mother lode of personal expression—the one place in our lives that we (as people lucky enough to have access) can say whatever we want about anything we want. This was the anti-television. Digital democracy.

I believed that. And the crazy part is, I still do.

My first exposure to the idea of a "weblog" was about a year ago. I'd been visiting CamWorld[1] for years and I liked it. But the idea of calling it a genre baffled me. Link-plus-commentary didn't seem all that revolutionary to me.

Certainly not as revolutionary as Jon Katz made it out to be in his breathless write-up[2] of the trend in *Slashdot*. I read his words carefully, and I tried to believe. But I just couldn't see a revolution in personal expression and community in the robotic scrolling headlines of Robot Wisdom.[3]

By nature, I'm suspicious of hype. I think anyone with a journalism background is like that. And, given the tidal wave of hype weblogs received in late 1999, it was hard not to rebel. I started saying that I hated weblogs, just to see what would happen.

It was partly true. I did hate the hype[4] that weblogs got. Hype is ugly, and rarely good for the thing it's about. I also hated the exclusionary nature of the community that cropped up around weblogs. It's perfectly natural, of course, for people with like interests to congregate. But I've always tried to remain open to new people and new ideas. It seemed to me, as an outside observer, that the weblog community circled its wagons almost immediately.

Finally, I hated the fact that the essence of weblogging at that time, and perhaps still today, was the off-site link. A witty quip, a link away, updated as much as possible. It was easy (and predictable) to foresee a future Web of "independent content" that consisted solely of pointing at people who are pointing at other people. All of a sudden, there was no more there.

I always wanted to see people make things. Big,[5] beautiful,[6] daring[7] things. Not yet another pointer to yet another *Salon* article.

So I did something dreadful. Something despicable. Something so horrible and evil I couldn't stand the sight of myself in the mirror in the morning. I started weblogging.

I figured, if I wanted to understand it, I should just try it. And besides, powazek.com was already set up for daily updates. I had been using it to post the news of the Powazek Productions (fray, kvetch, and sfstories). There was really very little difference between what I was doing already, and a weblog. So I dipped my toe in the water. Slowly.

And I felt that virus all over again.

As soon as I began posting every day, I started getting email. The voices were friendly, and encouraging. My hits rose steadily, and people started to link back.

But what's more, I found I had a forum for the voices in my head that didn't fit anywhere else. I had plenty of places to tell the big stories[8] of my life. But the little, fleeting thoughts now had a home, too. It even encouraged a sense of goofy fun[9] I'd never expressed on the Web before.

I was hooked. "Weblogging," I told a friend over Jack-n-Cokes, "is fun."

And then, of course, came the dark side.

Neale[10] grouped a bunch of webloggers into high school cliques and called me a jock,[11] which would be hysterical to anyone who knew me in high school. It could have been an interesting commentary on the dangers of clique-ism in the weblog community, but to me it just came off as mean. You could almost hear Nelson cackling, "Ha ha!"

Then Dave[12] decided I must be "brain-damaged" because I used frames. As if there was One Right Way to do a weblog and I had violated it, so he should mock me into compliance. It was a mean-spirited, overtly personal attack.

This is the dark side of weblogging I'd feared. It saddens me because, over the last year, weblogging really matured as a genre. And as a community. We should strive to stay true to the inclusive nature of the web. We should be welcoming and encouraging to new voices and ideas, because, in the end, that's how the Web evolves.

The Web isn't about rules and my-way-or-the-highway ideologies, remember? The fun thing about the Web is that it's still so new. We're still making it up! And innovation comes from people who do things a little differently. Anyone who forgets that and clings to narrow-minded ideologies will take their rightful place in a forgotten history.

So here we are. I've been running a weblog for almost six months (or over a year, depending on when you start counting). And the good still outweighs the bad. In fact, I'm ready to finally say it:

I don't hate weblogs. I love weblogs. Honest.

I love weblogs because they're yet another way for people to express themselves online. Sure, they're full of links. They're also full of lives. Look at the way Meg[13] uploads her train of thought on a daily basis, or Tom[14] tells us about his love life, or Jack[15] tells his stories. These are real people, putting their lives online.

Diary. Weblog. Portal. Blah. You can call it whatever you want. Just don't stop doing it.

I'll most likely continue to log the things that are new with the Powazek Productions here, as well as link to things that I'm interested in. If you find it interesting, I'm glad. Drop me a line and say hi.

And if you don't, that's fine, too. Maybe you should start one[16] of your own.

Weblogs: A History and Perspective

Rebecca Blood
September 7, 2000

IN 1998 THERE WERE JUST A HANDFUL OF SITES OF THE TYPE THAT are now identified as weblogs (so named by Jorn Barger[1] in December 1997). Jesse James Garrett, editor of Infosift,[2] began compiling a list of "other sites like his" as he found them in his travels around the Web. In November of that year, he sent that list to Cameron Barrett. Cameron published the list on CamWorld,[3] and others maintaining similar sites began sending their URLs to him for inclusion on the list. Jesse's "page of only weblogs"[4] lists the 23 known to be in existence at the beginning of 1999.

Suddenly a community sprang up. It was easy to read all of the weblogs on Cameron's list, and most interested people did. Peter Merholz[5] announced in early 1999 that he was going to pronounce it "wee-blog" and inevitably this was shortened to "blog" with the weblog editor referred to as a "blogger."

At this point, the bandwagon jumping began. More and more people began publishing their own weblogs. I began mine in April of 1999. Suddenly it became difficult to read every weblog every day, or even to keep track of all the new ones that were appearing. Cameron's list grew so large that he began including only weblogs he actually followed himself. Other webloggers did the same. In early 1999, Brigitte Eaton[6] compiled a list of every weblog she knew about and created the Eatonweb Portal.[7] Brig evaluated all submissions by a simple criterion: that the site consist of dated entries. Webloggers debated what was and what was not a weblog, but since the Eatonweb Portal was the most complete listing of weblogs available, Brig's inclusive definition prevailed.

This rapid growth continued steadily until July 1999 when Pitas,[8] the first free build-your-own-weblog tool launched, and suddenly there were hundreds. In August, Pyra[9] released Blogger, and Groksoup[10] launched, and with the ease that these Web-based tools provided, the bandwagon-jumping turned into an explosion. Late in 1999, software developer Dave Winer introduced Edit This Page,[11] and Jeff A. Campbell launched Velocinews. All of these services are free, and all of them are designed to enable individuals to publish their own weblogs quickly and easily.

The original weblogs were link-driven sites. Each was a mixture in unique proportions of links, commentary, and personal thoughts and essays. Weblogs could only be created by people who already knew how to make a website. A weblog editor had either taught herself to code HTML for fun, or, after working all day creating commercial websites, spent several off-work hours every day surfing the Web and posting to her site. These were Web enthusiasts.

Many current weblogs follow this original style. Their editors present links both to little-known corners of the Web and to current news articles they feel are worthy of note. Such links are nearly always accompanied by the editor's commentary. An editor with some expertise in a field might demonstrate the accuracy or inaccuracy of a highlighted article or certain facts therein; provide additional facts he feels are pertinent to the issue at hand; or simply add an opinion or differing viewpoint from the one in the piece he has linked. Typically this commentary is characterized by an irreverent, sometimes sarcastic tone. More skillful editors manage to convey all of these things in the sentence or two with which they introduce the link (making them, as Halcyon[12] pointed out to me, pioneers in the art and craft of microcontent[13]). Indeed, the format of the typical weblog, providing only a very short space in which to write an entry, encourages pithiness on the part of the writer; longer commentary is often given its own space as a separate essay.

These weblogs provide a valuable filtering function for their readers. The Web has been, in effect, pre-surfed for them. Out of the myriad webpages slung through cyberspace, weblog editors pick out the most mind-boggling, the most stupid, the most compelling.

But this type of weblog is important for another reason, I think. In Douglas Rushkoff's *Media Virus*, Greg Ruggerio of the Immediast Underground[14] is quoted as saying, "Media is a corporate possession. . . . You cannot participate in the media. Bringing that into the foreground is the first step. The second step is to define the difference between public and audience. An audience is passive; a public is participatory. We need a definition of media that is public in its orientation."

By highlighting articles that may easily be passed over by the typical Web user too busy to do more than scan corporate news sites, by searching out articles from lesser-known sources, and by providing additional facts, alternative views, and thoughtful commentary, weblog editors participate in the dissemination and interpretation of the news that is fed to us every day. Their sarcasm and fearless commentary remind us to question the vested interests of our sources of information and the expertise of indi-

vidual reporters as they file news stories about subjects they may
not fully understand.

Weblog editors sometimes contextualize an article by juxtapos-
ing it with an article on a related subject; each article, considered
in the light of the other, may take on additional meaning, or even
draw the reader to conclusions contrary to the implicit aim of
each. It would be too much to call this type of weblog "independent media," but clearly their editors, engaged in seeking out and
evaluating the "facts" that are presented to us each day, resemble
the public that Ruggerio speaks of. By writing a few lines each
day, weblog editors begin to redefine media as a public, participatory endeavor.

Now during 1999, something else happened, and I believe it
has to do with the introduction of Blogger itself.

While weblogs had always included a mix of links, commentary, and personal notes, in the post-Blogger explosion increasing numbers of weblogs eschewed this focus on the Web-at-
large in favor of a sort of short-form journal. These blogs, often
updated several times a day, were instead a record of the blogger's thoughts: something noticed on the way to work, notes
about the weekend, a quick reflection on some subject or another. Links took the reader to the site of another blogger with
whom the first was having a public conversation or had met the
previous evening, or to the site of a band he had seen the night
before. Full-blown conversations were carried on between three
or five blogs, each referencing the other in their agreement or
rebuttal of the other's positions. Cults of personality sprung up
as new blogs appeared, certain names appearing over and over
in daily entries or listed in the obligatory sidebar of "other
weblogs" (a holdover from Cam's original list). It was, and is,
fascinating to see new bloggers position themselves in this community, referencing and reacting to those blogs they read most,

their sidebar an affirmation of the tribe to which they wish to belong.

Why the change? Why so many? I have always suspected that some of the popularity of this form may be a simple desire to emulate the sites of head Pyra kids Ev[15] and Meg.[16] As the creators of Blogger, their charming, witty blogs are their company's foremost advertisement for its most popular product.

More than that, Blogger itself places no restrictions on the form of content being posted. Its Web interface, accessible from any browser, consists of an empty form box into which the blogger can type . . . anything: a passing thought, an extended essay, or a childhood recollection. With a click, Blogger will post the . . . whatever . . . on the writer's website, archive it in the proper place, and present the writer with another empty box, just waiting to be filled.

Contrast this with the Web interface of MetaFilter,[17] a popular community weblog. Here, the writer is presented with three form boxes: the first for the URL of the referenced site, the second for the title of the entry, and the third for whatever commentary the writer would like to add. The MetaFilter interface instructs the writer to contribute a link and add commentary; Blogger makes no such demands. Blogger makes it so easy to type in a thought or reaction that many people are disinclined to hunt up a link and compose some text around it.

It is this free-form interface combined with absolute ease of use which has, in my opinion, done more to impel the shift from the filter-style weblog to journal-style blog than any other factor. And there has been a shift. Searching for a filter-style weblog by clicking through the thousands of weblogs listed at weblogs.com,[18] the Eatonweb Portal,[19] or Blogger Directory[20] can be a Sisyphean task. Newcomers would appear to be most drawn to the blog— rather than filter—style of weblogging.

Certainly, both styles still exist; certainly the particular mixture of links, commentary, and personal observation unique to each individual site has always given each weblog its distinctive voice and personality; and certainly the weblog has always been an infinitely malleable format. But the influx of blogs has changed the definition of weblog from "a list of links with commentary and personal asides" to "a website that is updated frequently, with new material posted at the top of the page." I really wish there were another term to describe the filter-style weblog, one that would easily distinguish it from the blog. On the principle of truth in advertising, this would make it much easier for the adventuresome reader to find the type of weblog he most enjoys.

So, what of the weblog? Is it of interest or importance to anyone who does not produce one? Well, I think it should be.

A filter-style weblog provides many advantages to its readers. It reveals glimpses of an unimagined Web to those who have no time to surf. An intelligent human being filters through the mass of information packaged daily for our consumption and picks out the interesting, the important, the overlooked, and the unexpected. This human being may provide additional information to that which corporate media provides, expose the fallacy of an argument, perhaps reveal an inaccurate detail. Because the weblog editor can comment freely on what she finds, one week of reading will reveal to you her personal biases, making her a predictable source. This further enables us to turn a critical eye to both the information and comments she provides. Her irreverent attitude challenges the veracity of the "facts" presented each day by authorities.

Shortly after I began producing Rebecca's Pocket, I noticed two side effects I had not expected. First, I discovered my own interests. I thought I knew what I was interested in, but after linking stories for a few months, I could see that I was much more interested in science, archaeology, and issues of injustice than I had realized. More importantly, I began to value more highly my own point of view. In composing my linktext every day I carefully considered my own opinions and ideas, and I began to feel that my perspective was unique and important.

This profound experience may be most purely realized in the blog-style weblog. Lacking a focus on the outside world, the blogger is compelled to share his world with whomever is reading. He may engage other bloggers in conversation about the interests they share. He may reflect on a book he is reading, or the behavior of someone on the bus. He might describe a flower that he saw growing between the cracks of a sidewalk on his way to work. Or he may simply jot notes about his life: what work is like, what he had for dinner, what he thought of a recent movie. These fragments, pieced together over months, can provide an unexpectedly intimate view of what it is to be a particular individual in a particular place at a particular time.

The blogger, by virtue of simply writing down whatever is on his mind, will be confronted with his own thoughts and opinions. Blogging every day, he will become a more confident writer. A community of 100 or 20 or 3 people may spring up around the public record of his thoughts. Being met with friendly voices, he may gain more confidence in his view of the world; he may begin to experiment with longer forms of writing, to play with haiku, or to begin a creative project—one that he would have dismissed as being inconsequential or doubted he could complete only a few months before.

As he enunciates his opinions daily, this new awareness of his inner life may develop into a trust in his own perspective. His own reactions—to a poem, to other people, and, yes, to the media—will carry more weight with him. Accustomed to expressing his thoughts on his website, he will be able to more fully articulate his opinions to himself and others. He will become impatient with waiting to see what others think before he decides, and will begin to act in accordance with his inner voice instead. Ideally, he will become less reflexive and more reflective, and find his own opinions and ideas worthy of serious consideration.

His readers will remember an incident from their own childhood when the blogger relates a memory. They might look more closely at the other riders on the train after the blogger describes his impressions of a fellow commuter. They will click back and forth between blogs and analyze each blogger's point of view in a multi-blog conversation, and form their own conclusions on the matter at hand. Reading the views of other ordinary people, they will readily question and evaluate what is being said. Doing this, they may begin a similar journey of self-discovery and intellectual self-reliance.

The promise of the Web was that everyone could publish, that a thousand voices could flourish, communicate, connect. The truth was that only those people who knew how to code a webpage could make their voices heard. Blogger, Pitas, and all the rest have given people with little or no knowledge of HTML the ability to publish on the Web: to pontificate, remember, dream, and argue in public, as easily as they send an instant message. We can't seriously compare the creation of the World Wide Web itself with the availability of free technology that allows anyone with a Web browser to express their unique, irreproducible vision to the rest of the world . . . can we?

In September of 2000 there are thousands of weblogs: topic-oriented weblogs, alternative viewpoints, astute examinations of the human condition as reflected by mainstream media, short-form journals, links to the weird, and free-form notebooks of ideas. Traditional weblogs perform a valuable filtering service and provide tools for more critical evaluation of the information available on the Web. Free-style blogs are nothing less than an outbreak of self-expression. Each is evidence of a staggering shift from an age of carefully controlled information provided by sanctioned authorities (and artists) to an unprecedented opportunity for individual expression on a worldwide scale. Each kind of weblog empowers individuals on many levels.

So why doesn't every bookmark list contain five weblogs? In the beginning of 1999, it really seemed that by now every bookmark list would. There was a bit of media attention and new weblogs were being created every day. It was a small, quick-growing community and it seemed to be on the edge of a wider awareness. Perhaps the tsunami of new weblogs created in the wake of Pitas and Blogger crushed the movement before it could reach critical mass; the sudden exponential growth of the community rendered it unnavigable. Weblogs, once filters of the Web, suddenly became so numerous they were as confusing as the Web itself. A few more articles appeared touting weblogs as the next big thing. But the average reader, hopefully clicking through to the Eatonweb portal, found herself faced with an alphabetical list of a thousand weblogs. Not knowing where to begin, she quickly retreated back to ABCnews.com.

I don't have an answer. In our age, the single-page website of an obscure Turk named Mahir can sweep the Web in days. But the unassailable truth is that corporate media and commercial and governmental entities own most of the real estate. Dell manages more webpages than all of the weblogs put together. Sprite's PR machine can point more man-hours to the promotion of one message—"Obey Your Thirst"—than the combined man-hours of every weblogger alive. Our strength—that each of us speaks in an individual voice of an individual vision—is, in the high-stakes world of carefully orchestrated messages designed to distract and manipulate, a liability. We are, very simply, outnumbered.

And what, really, will change if we get weblogs into every bookmark list? As we are increasingly bombarded with information from our computers, handhelds, in-store kiosks, and now our clothes, the need for reliable filters will become more pressing. As corporate interests exert tighter and tighter control over information and even art, critical evaluation is more essential than ever. As advertisements creep onto banana peels, attach themselves to paper cup sleeves, and interrupt our ATM transactions, we urgently need to cultivate forms of self-expression in order to counteract our self-defensive numbness and remember what it is to be human.

We are being pummeled by a deluge of data and unless we create time and spaces in which to reflect, we will be left with only our reactions. I strongly believe in the power of weblogs to transform both writers and readers from "audience" to "public" and from "consumer" to "creator." Weblogs are no panacea for the crippling effects of a media-saturated culture, but I believe they are one antidote.

Here Come the Weblogs

Jon Katz

May 24, 2001

Weblogs, described by one of their creators as the "pirate radio stations" of the Web, are a new, personal, and determinedly non-hostile evolution of the electric community. They are also the freshest example of how people use the Net to make their own radically different new media. A look at weblogs plus a list of a few identifiable existing species in the electric community. Feel free, of course, to add your own.

Electric Community Part Two:

The members of electronic communities like *Slashdot* come together in the first place because of some shared interest—in this case a complex, sometimes highly technical range of acquired knowledge—Linux, open source, programming. An individualistic community with a common purpose, sites like this attract focused, like-minded participants, programmers and developers whose shared experience was mastery of a complex operating system, a willingness to endure technical hurdles, and an almost secret common language.

Newcomers, drawn to see what's going on or foraging for information themselves, often enrage the established dwellers of an e-community. They don't know as much, ask stupid questions, speak a different language. Intruders, they throw the ecological balance out of whack.

Mark Stefik of the Information Sciences and Technology Laboratory at the Xerox Palo Alto Research Center, likens this resentment to the problem of assimilation when natural disasters or wars cause mass exodus to new lands. When the rate of immigration exceeds a certain level, the resulting chaos in the host country can evoke tremendous resentment and backlash.

Size is a factor, too. As an electric community grows, so do the maintenance costs—hardware, bandwidth, the pressure to present coherently more and more information, the need for revenue to support all these functions. As more and more people move through the site, it's harder to recognize addresses, message styles, or individual personalities.

So an electronic community faces, from the beginning, a serious dilemma—whether to stay small, but remain marginal, or to grow, and become more profitable and acquire more bandwidth and software. In a sense, it suffers either way. If a community stays small, it starves. If it grows, it suffers in a different way. The WELL, one of the first and most important electronic communities (I've been a member for years) has survived by remaining small, smart, and simple.

Many of its members have reasons for avoiding too much hostility. They have continuing, powerful, very personal ties to one another. Topics range from science and technology to culture, movies, and parenting. And the WELL has been successful in part by providing strong, experienced moderators with authority who discourage eruptions of hostility and keep conversations on track without discouraging free speech.

E-communities without personal forums—jobs, parenting, family life—have a tougher time forming a sense of community, since there's no real way for members to get to know one another. People aren't attacking human beings they know, but disembodied voices and messages.

From the beginning, the Net and the Web have been about individuals creating their own media. This process evolves constantly as people online struggle to find communities where they can glean information, keep up with new technologies, receive help, make human contact.

Some online sociologists use the club analogy when it comes to differentiating large and public versus small and exclusive e-communities.

Exclusive discussion groups—those that limit membership and topics—are like private clubs in that they offer membership by invitation or even fees. In these smaller e-communities, people can speak more freely, perhaps say things they wouldn't say in public.

Stefik writes: "To take the private-club idea another step forward, consider the possibility of private clubs with exclusive memberships, rules about confidentiality with real bite, and limits on the ability of the excluded public to post. There might be private newsgroups for people who are generally inaccessible; for example, major financiers, philanthropists, leaders of powerful companies, or even scientists."

The recent surge in classy, well-designed, intensely linked weblogs—almost all, essentially reflecting the interests and tastes of their creators and a small number of like-minded people—suggests a non-commercial version on Stefik's idea.

The weblog isn't a new term on the Net, but it's being used in a new way. One previous definition of weblog is an archive of activity on a Web server. Another is an online diary. But in the context of the e-community, the weblog is new, and evolving rapidly, despite the fact that specialized and idiosyncratic sites have been around for some years.

On camworld.com,[1] Cameron Barrett has written about and developed his notion of the weblog—he calls it a small, eclectic site, usually maintained by one person, with a high concentration of repeat visitors, plentiful WWW links, and a zero tolerance for flames.

Barrett, an interactive designer, writes on CamWorld ("Anatomy of a Weblog"[2]) that he heard the term "weblog" for the first time a few months ago, but isn't sure who coined it.

Weblogs are a perfect example of the biological evolution of electronic communities. Very personal foraging sites, they are limited in membership, their links continuously updated, and are often focused on a single subject or theme.

They seem to almost all be ideologically opposed to hostility, including essayish commentary and observations. Because the site creator limits and approves membership, they don't need to be defended as intensely as bigger sites, nor do they attract—or permit—posters who abuse others. One obvious payoff is that the flow of ideas is strong, uninterrupted, and impressive.

Barrett calls weblogs "microportals." Some weblogs: Smug;[3] Flutterby;[4] Scripting News;[5] Robot Wisdom;[6] Stating the Obvious[7]—I was startled to come upon a column by Rogers Cadenhead about why I don't belong on *Slashdot* (weblogs may be less hostile, but don't look for sweet, either); Obscure Store,[8] and Joshua Eli Schachter's very smart Memepool.[9]

Some webpools are designed by their creators simply to revolve around what they find interesting. Writer Keith Dawson describes webpools as "filtered news," but as with anything having to do with the Net and the Web, there are lots of different points of view.

The *Christian Science Monitor* newspaper, emails Christine Booker, was "weblogging" their own publication earlier this week.[10] That is, an editor provided synopses of articles of interest, with links and particularly notable quotes. The editor was providing pre-digested highlights of his paper, only without commentary. Thus "weblogging" has even come to journalism, not usually an institution on the forefront of digital change.

The point is, Booker wrote, instead of asking readers to scan headlines to decide what to read, they have a section at the top of their World Report that says, in effect: our international editor puts foreign news coverage in perspective so that you can go straight to the meat. In a different way, that's what weblogs do— interesting stories for preselected communities.

Booker, who designs and manages websites for the University of Washington Department of Surgery and is an avid reader of weblogs, says it's important to convey their personal nature. "Even sites that don't contain any original content or much commentary give me a glimpse into the mind of the weblogger. What someone chooses to link tells me what they're interested in, what they think is funny, what they find absurd. Some webloggers offer links embedded in one or two lines of more or less oblique commentary." (jjg.net[11]) Booker says that as far as she can tell, many, if not most, of these sites started very informally and then, one way or another, the URL got passed around. Soon these "hobby sites" developed devoted audiences, readers who visit them at least daily, sometimes more often.

Jesse James Garrett, content editor for Ingram Micro's website and editor of the weblog jjg.net, says that "weblogs are the pirate radio stations of the Web, personal platforms through which individuals broadcast their perspectives on current events, the media, our culture, and basically anything else that strikes their fancy from the vast sea of raw material available out there on the

Web. Some are more topic-focused than others, but all are really built around someone's personal interests. Neither a faceless news-gathering organization nor an impersonal clipping service, a quality weblog is distinguished by the voice of its editor, and that editor's connection with his or her audience."

One of the best weblogs I found was Peter Merholz's peterme.com.[12] "How freakin' cool is this?" he asks in the lead item for May 12, writing about tracking satellites live and real-time using a 3D Java applet. The site mixes the best of Web design and technology—interface, design, Web development—with pop culture: movie reviews, an essay on the late cartoonist Shel Silverstein.

Merholz has decided, "for what it's worth," to pronounce "weblog" as "wee-blog."

While weblogs don't have the reach and influence—thus, the commercial potential—of larger, more interactive and open sites, it's easy to imagine them as powerful supplements to the major foraging sites. And, depending on their members, they could be influential at sharing memes, essays, and ideas.

Cameron Barrett's thoughts on weblogs can be found at http://www.camworld.com/journal/rants/99/01/26.html, along with his list of favorites. Keith Dawson, who runs the Tasty Bits of Technology Front site, in some ways a pioneer, classic weblog, also has written about weblogs at http://www.tbtf.com/archive/current-issue.html.

To me, weblogs may embody personalized media on the Net—enterprising geeks creating interesting new sites that set out to define news in different ways, to be both interesting, coherent, and more civil. This is the complete opposite structure of conventional media, which is top-down, boring, and inherently arrogant.

They may be among the first e-communities to successfully overcome online hostility and abuse as well. That alone could make them highly popular.

Weblogs, however personal, are foraging sites in the classic sense of the term.

But weblogs aside, the idea of electronic communities as encompassing distinct biological types is irresistible. And it makes sense. I'd identify these species of electric villagers. Add your own:

FORAGERS (Stefik would call them Wolves): The people running sites or submitting and linking to discovered information.

LURKERS (Stefik's Spiders): The largest group, professionals, academics, researchers and others, whose need for information is practical, and who wait for it, usually in silence.

FISHERMEN: People who trawl selected sub-topics or discussions for specific data, such as information about a kind of information or software.

HELPERS: Electronic communities often have a contingent of knowledgeable veterans who welcome newcomers, and are happy to counsel them in the ways of the site. The helpers don't see newcomers as a threat, but an opportunity for the village to grow and prosper.

IDEOLOGISTS (as in priests and theologists): Vigilant for deviations from what they perceive as the site's purpose, they disagree and criticize, sometimes sharply, but rarely with venom or cruelty.

DEFENDERS (as in warrior bees or ants): Ideologically driven flamers who seek to keep their communities pure, free from intrusive outsiders, whom they see as threatening and destabilizing.

ANONYMOUS COWARDS (Spies, informers, information bringers and Braying Hyenas): Two types, people with legitimate information that they can't share under their own names, and ex hibitionists who get to express hostility without consequence. The single biggest cause of the destruction of communities, they are the most frequently cited reason newcomers flee, veterans tire, and advertisers move on to more hospitable environments.

TECHS (worker bees and ants): The people in any community for whom the construction of the site is its own reward. They are constantly working to offer options and services, improve software and access.

Some questions: What does an electric community need to work? Are there other identifiable types of e-community members? Are new kinds of sites like weblogs the future, or a minor step on the evolutionary chain?

Anatomy of a Weblog

Cameron Barrett

January 26, 1999

WEBLOG.

A few months back, I heard the term *weblog* for the first time. I'm not sure who coined it or where it came from, so I can't properly credit it. Typically, a weblog is a small website, usually maintained by one person that is updated on a regular basis and has a high concentration of repeat visitors. Weblogs often are highly focused around a singular subject, an underlying theme or unifying concept.

I asked on my own personal website, "Is CamWorld a weblog?" A guy named Michal[1] (Sabren) answered. "Yep."

I stood back a few steps and realized that yeah, CamWorld is a weblog or a *microportal*. It's got all of the aspects commonly associated with weblogs. It's updated regularly [daily]. It's got a nice, clean easy-to-use design and user interface. It doesn't patronize to the end user, dumbing things down too much. It has a theme [Random Thoughts + Web Design + New Media]. It has a way for the users to interact with each other [a mailing list[2]]. It even has somewhat of a community, maintained by repeat visitors and list members who contribute many of the links often found in CamWorld.

Most weblog owners are aware of each other and make it a point to credit the source of a particularly amusing or useful link. I often find it's not even necessary to credit a popular link, especially if I see it turn up on other weblogs and websites. It's also not necessary to credit a link to a news article from a major news source, as most weblog owners use many of the same news sources for their usual links.

One of the largest and most useful weblogs I've ever seen is Jorn Barger's Robot Wisdom Weblog.[3] How he has the time to find all of these daily links, I do not know. I often find it quite hard to keep CamWorld updated every day, as I'm fully employed and treat CamWorld as a hobby site, mostly updated between 10:00 P.M. and midnight the night before, where publishing typically occurs around midnight of a new day (EST).

A different kind of weblog (one that has multiple contributors) is Joshua Schachter's Memepool,[4] a site that is updated by approved contributors. Each contributed entry is approved by the editor before being posted. The biggest potential problem with a site like this is that if the pool of contributors gets too large, the number of daily postings can become too large for the editor to handle. Regardless, this may be the only good way for a weblog to exist, as it effectively distributes the workload among numerous people.

Some weblogs are updated only on weekdays and often feature only one or two high-quality links a day. A good example of this is Jesse James Garrett's jjg.net.[5] Jesse spends his days as the content editor for the Ingram Micro website. Another example is Dan Lyke's Flutterby.[6] Dan works as a software engineer for Pixar.

Which leads me into an interesting corollary. Most weblog editors/owners work full-time in the Internet industry. Most have many years of proven Internet research skills that they utilize every day. Michael Sippey of Stating the Obvious[7] calls this process filtering, and his now-defunct Filter was another early weblog.

It can be argued that Dave Winer's Scripting News[8] was the first successful weblog on the Internet, fuelled by his popular newsletter DaveNet, published regularly since 1994. A site that I've followed for many years, Scripting News offers daily links to industry news, technology news, funny pictures, opinions, and other completely fascinating tidbits. CamWorld is openly modeled after Scripting News, just as Wesley Felter's Hacking the Planet[9] is modeled after CamWorld.

Another interesting observation about weblogs is the percentage of them being maintained by a software package called Userland Frontier.[10] Not coincidentally, Dave Winer of Scripting News is the creator and developer behind Frontier. Other technologies behind weblogs are various scripting languages like php3, Perl, and Python.

Lastly, one of the best weblogs currently in production is Jim Romanesko's Obscure Store.[11] Jim, a seasoned journalist, has a very firm grasp on the world of online journalism. Not a day goes by that I can't find at least two articles from his site that are worthy of reading.

In some sense, weblogs sum up what's so great about the Internet. Like fanzine editors before them, weblog editors embrace a topic or theme and run with it. Weblogs are a great indicator of what's happening on the Internet and within the Web community. As our weblogs grow and mature, let's offer up some hope for those that follow in our footsteps. Pass along your tips for finding the best tidbits and links. Archive your site and make it searchable. Run a link-checking program against it to combat link-rot, and occasionally dig through your archives to find the truly great links, and feature them again.

But most important of all, don't forget to have fun.

More About Weblogs

Cameron Barrett
May 11, 1999

FOR NEARLY A YEAR NOW, I'VE SPENT ONE TO THREE HOURS EVERY night surfing the Web, reading everything I came across, judging the quality of the writing and information, and determining whether or not my readers would be interested in the same things I was. The truth is, I'm burning out. I wonder if I can do this anymore.

I need to slow down a little and try to write more commentary, more essays, and focus less on trying to serve up as many quality links as I could manage. Instead of visiting every day as some of you faithfully have, swing on by every second or third day to see if I've added anything.

In the long run, I believe that this is what you all want. Less senseless hype. Less gratuitous linking. Less focus on the sensationalistic journalism that's crowding our brains and turning them into mush. More focus on the truly exceptional content out there on the Web that only a few of us manage to dig up. More personal essays. More professional essays. And yes, even the occasional rant.

You see, CamWorld is about me. It's about who I am, what I know, and what I think. And it's about my place in the New

28

Media society. CamWorld is a peek into the subconsciousness that makes me tick. It's not about finding the most links the fastest, automated archiving, or searchable personal websites. It's about educating those who have come to know me about what I feel is important in the increasingly complex world we live in, both online and off.

CamWorld is an experiment in self-expression. And that experiment is not over. Over the next year (or two or three), CamWorld will evolve into something more. It will always have its loyal readers just as Stephen King and his publishing house have millions of people committed to buying his next book (regardless of whether it sucks or not). CamWorld grew from a little site built to support a new media college class I was teaching into what it is today.

Maintaining a daily weblog is harder than it looks. I applaud those who manage to keep theirs updated daily, sometimes with too much material for even me to keep up with. The two that come immediately to mind are Jorn Barger's Robot Wisdom Weblog[1] and Lawrence Lee's Tomalak's Realm.[2] While the former sports plenty of opinionated commentary and dozens of links every day, the latter is a headline aggregator with pullquotes. That doesn't make it any less useful, though. On the contrary, some headline aggregator sites (often mistaken for weblogs) are very useful for reviewing what's happening on the Web on any given day.

Lately, there has been an explosion of growth in the weblog community. In some ways, I detest this growth, as it makes my efforts with CamWorld even harder. Some have criticized the weblog format and labeled it the "latest Internet craze." Others have dismissed it as nothing more than people rediscovering the power of a quality home page. I disagree. Home pages are places where you put pictures of your family and your cats. It's a place to distribute information to a close circle of family and friends.

Weblogs, however, are designed for an audience. They have a voice. They have a personality. Simply put, they are an interactive extension of who you are.

In short, the weblog is here to stay, regardless of whether it's updated daily, weekly, or whenever the owner damn well feels like it. And that's the point. Newspapers have daily deadlines because they have a committed (and paying) daily audience. Magazines have weekly and monthy deadlines because they too have a committed (and paying) audience who expects them to publish on time. Keep in mind that weblogs have their own established audiences who expect certain things from each owner. The last thing you should expect, however, is for them to cater to your every whim. That's simply a very selfish expectation and shouldn't be tolerated.

I hope the weblog "craze" continues as more and more people discover the power of a regularly updated site that reflects their own unique personality. In a few years, it'd be neat to see the weblog format overtake the standard home page format with GIFs of people's cats, dogs, babies, and cars. But I doubt it will happen. It's taken us almost six years to get people to understand that home pages don't need to have every funny little GIF animation they've ever seen, or silly javascript rollovers, or even that browser-crashing Java pong game. Focus more on the content and less on the glitz. As the Internet community and Geocities members realize that the reasons they've had only 102 hits on their page(s) in a year (100 of them from their own IP address), the quality of their online initiatives will go up as they begin to understand what is required to keep a regular audience happy and well-fed with information.

I know, I know . . . I've rambled on too long, but some of these scattered thoughts have been cluttering up my brain for far too long. So bear with me, as I do a little housecleaning up top.

I'd like to address an issue that has bothered me for some time. It's about crediting a source online within a weblog. Out of a common courtesy, I (and many other weblog owners) usually give credit to a site where we first saw the article, story, quote, or tidbit we're linking to. There are two different camps of this thinking: those who think crediting initial sources is good, and those who don't. Several weblogs have developed a system where a source is credited with an acronym, and then somewhere else there is a key that explains the acronym system to the reader who is interested enough to dig that deep. Robot Wisdom and Card-house[3] are examples of weblogs that do this, with [cw] being the acronym for CamWorld at the latter. Other sites simply add a short credit like [via Flutterby[4]] or [found at Obscure Store[5]] after each link.

I like the idea of crediting an initial source, but wonder if it clutters up the flow of information a weblog is trying to deliver. As a weblog editor, I encourage the idea of crediting a source, as it informs each weblog's audience about other potential sources of information they might enjoy. Along this same vein of thought, it's discomforting to see some weblogs (or headline aggregators) simply compile a list of links culled from a list of weblogs they frequent every day.

The "big idea" of the Internet is the power of distributed information where anyone can, with a little hard work, develop a website that hundreds and thousands of people may want to read and/or participate in. Seeing that hard work being lever-aged on another site without proper credit tends to get me down. And rightly so. The Internet is about personalized and customized communication. Weblogs have established a small island of rationality and stability among the sea of information that the Internet has thrown at everyone. Those of us who are honing our skills at filtering this information are creating the best weblogs. The better the signal-to-noise ratio, the better your site will be.

I'm still waiting for the weblog model to be adopted by others. Woudn't it be great if all the neurosurgeons in the world had one place to go for up-to-date information about the numerous changes in their field? (This could be a subscription-only site!) Or what about government-centric weblogs? The FCC has a Daily Digest[6] mailing list that attempts to keep the public up-to-date on all of their changing regulations, but it's simply not the same as a weblog as it has no attached personality or voice.

Every industry in the world has a potential need for a quality weblog or two. It's safe to say that the Macintosh community has been inundated with Mac-centric news sites for several years now. So many, that I've lost count. But what about a weblog for the homemaker? Or the thousands of hot rod enhusiasts? Or the ham radio hobbyists? These are called niche market portals, and every one of them (and thousands of other niche markets) could be a potential source of quality information for someone.

The closest thing to this model I've seen is the Mining Company[7] (now About.com). They have an infrastructure of about 500 mini-sites or so that focus on some of the more popular niche markets on the Internet. They pay editors to keep these sites updated on a regular basis. The only reason I think they are not well-known is the lack of a great advertising campaign, the absence of the infamous Internet hype about them, and a general lack of awareness among the millions of Internet users who could benefit from the information they are compiling and distributing.

Another interesting application of the weblog model would be within corporate intranets. Where I work, much of the company-wide memorandums and communication are done via email, with some emails containing numerous attachments that sometimes weigh in at a hefty one-to-two megabytes. It'd be so much better if these emails only referenced documents somewhere on the intranet instead of including them via attachments. The intranet page for each department could be a regularly updated weblog of information currently being circulated. This would solve so many problems with disk space and deleted emails.

I hope that you all continue to visit CamWorld, and I hope that I've encouraged you to continue with your own weblogs. And if you don't have a weblog, then consider building one for your specific industry, specialty, or occupation. The world is in need of more specialized weblogs.

Go forth and blog.

6

Why I Weblog:
A Rumination on Where the Hell
I'm Going with This Website

Brad L. Graham

June 16, 1999

ABOUT A YEAR AGO, I TOOK THE PLUNGE AND SET UP MY OWN DOMAIN name. It was a practical decision, the result of having been buffeted from ISP to ISP by poor customer service, busy signals, and escalating service fees. I felt the need to have a static email address that I could feel safe printing on stationery and carry with me in my nomadic quest for the perfect provider.

After electing to register "bradlands.com,"[1] the urge to publish on the Net returned in spades. I've had a personal site called "The BradLands" off and on for six or seven years, since I first dipped my toe in the waters of HTML using America Online's[2] clunky FTP space to serve a few vanity pages.

The BradLands have (has?) been, by turns:

- a fairly typical and boring home page, outlining my interest, with obligatory links to some "cool sites" and with pictures of my friends;
- a somewhat more ambitious attempt to collect all of my writings, online and off, in one linked space;

- a poorly realized city guide to my fair city, St. Louis, back when there were few others;
- and, finally, the personal home page again, showing severe signs of infrequent updating and terminal link rot.

But here I was with a brand-new domain name and a need to show it off. I've always been prone to publishing in one form or another. An early indicator of my predisposition for journalism can be found among my parents' scrapbooks: it's a two page "family newsletter" I wrote longhand on legal paper when I was four or five years old, photocopied on my mom's mammoth IBM copier and distributed to interested readers.

Total circulation: two. Mom. Dad. Well, color me a magnate.

A few months before I threw up my hands and uttered a few colorful curses when my then-provider's local POP pooped out for the umpteenth time, I had started reading Steve Bogart's personal website, News, Pointers and Commentary[3] (now NowThis[4]).

Steve used to perform in an a capella group called MACH 1.[5] I saw them perform one night at Washington University, then checked out their site when I got home. His personal site was linked from there, and I discovered we had some common interests. His main page was updated frequently, in a fashion called "news page" or "web log," so I checked back from time to time and enjoyed his pointers to other web reading and his personal "scribbles" about computing issues and other topics. (A side note: for those of you keeping score at home, I've been reading Steve's page for more than a year. He works right down the street from me. We've never met, and have only just started a little email correspondence. It's a small world sometimes. And sometimes, it's a wide one too. [grin])

From Steve's page, I followed a link to Jorn Barger's Robot Wisdom Weblog,[6] and Jorn's page led me to Raphael Carter's

Honeyguide[7] and . . . well, from there the trail gets a little murky. Suffice it to say, I started reading these weblogs regularly and, eventually, decided to start one of my own.

The BradLands, version 3.0 (or so) was born, June 1998.

The early style of my weblog was wholly aped (OK, stolen) from Steve's page: a quote du jour, a few links, now and then a rant. As I continued to write for myself and audience of two or three readers a day, I also explored other sites that were maintaining similar pages.

Even though I was not, like Steve and Jorn, using Frontier[8] to maintain my site, I became a regular reader of Dave Winer's Scripting News.[9] I discovered Cameron Barrett's CamWorld,[10] Peter Merholz's PeterMe,[11] Lawrence Lee's Tomalak's Realm,[12] and Bill Humphries' More Like This.[13]

And, in the recent revamp of The BradLands, I borrowed (OK, stole) extensively from each of them to create the format I use today.

The BradLands still has a weblog; it's the page you're greeted with when you visit bradlands.com.[14] I've added sections for my old published writing (incomplete, but growing), my new Web-based essays, my current and all-time favorite books, and a few other bits I've yet to develop. Laurel Krahn, proprietor of the "Homicide: Life on the Street"-centric Minneapolis-based Windowseat[15] called what I do a "web home" when she noted its appearance in her own weblog. I suppose that's as apt a description of The BradLands as any.

But at the heart of it—posted right on the front door—is my weblog, infrequent though it may be, updating readers (now numbering about 60 per day) about projects I'm working on, links I find interesting, topics for discussion.

As The BradLands grew over the last year, more and more folks have started weblogs of their own, some with specific topics around which they focus, others more general in nature. There's a whole category for the breed in NewHoo[16] and other Web directories are taking note of the "weblog phenomenon."

At the same time, there's been some navel-gazing among those of us who maintain these sorts of pages, pondering why we do what we do the way we do it. Some folks have tried to define just what comprises a weblog; the definitions range narrow to wide. Cam had one of the better,[17] I thought.

Rather than add my voice to the fray and debate what is and is not a proper weblog, or to contemplate what purpose such a thing might serve for the Web community at large, I've been thinking about why I do it. Whether I'll continue. What shape The BradLands will take if I do.

Call it "The BradLand Manifesto," or, if you like, "Why I Weblog":

The aforementioned need to publish: I get off on seeing my words in print. My first byline in a daily newspaper almost made me wet myself with glee. More than that, I like the notion of leaving my words behind—even given the relatively ephemeral nature of the web—for others to find and enjoy.

A desire to minimize "fram": About the 15th time I received forwarded email about "Why the Internet is like a penis" or a plea for a terminally ill child who wants to receive greeting cards to make a world's record, I vowed never ever to forward a joke, petition, or other long-winded email to my entire address book. I get about 20 pieces of mail like this every day, often the same thing from several different folks around the country. (A wry observer called this propagation of forwarded mail "fram," a coinage denoting "spam from friends.") Instead of blindly cc'ing everyone I know, if I think it's worthy of passing on, I try to track down the original source on the Web ('cause it's there somewhere!) and either post the URL in my weblog or email just one or two folks I know who'll truly to be interested. As a result, I don't clutter my friends' in-boxes, and folks who know me well also know they can check out my website to see if anything truly noteworthy has come my way.

An opportunity to learn: This isn't strictly a motivation for my weblog, but it's a happy consequence. I got my first taste of HTML and web publishing during my brief stint as a tech writer. My first few pages were hand-coded in vi, and gave me a chance to learn the lingo from the ground up. Although these days, I tend to rely on WYSIWYG tools for most of the heavy-lifting, I'm still continuing to learn about markup by tweaking things by hand. I'm also getting some good insight into things such as how search engines work (or don't), how to grok JavaScript and—a leisurely summer provided—how to automate some stuff with scripting. I'm picking up cool skills in a pleasurable way that may have some real-world application down the line. A spoonful of sugar, and all that.

A license to explore: I spend a lot of time on the Internet, probably 2–3 hours a day all told reading for pleasure, maybe another hour or so on strictly work-related matters. I've more or less transferred my real-world habit of reading three newspapers a day to the web, only now I skim more like 25–30 publications regularly. I'm reading more and enjoying it. Still, using my weblog to link to stuff I've discovered in my surfing ameliorates some of my guilt about spending so much time in front of the screen. Surfing the Internet is fun, learning new things and discovering new resources is cool, and sharing the wealth with my weblog readers is a joy.

A sense of community: The first time I had a sense of the Internet as a place to convene a community was as a lurker and occasional poster on Usenet. As malicious and merely injudicious cross-posting unacceptably raised the newsgroup signal-to-noise ratio, I rediscovered that same feeling on a few, well-chosen email lists, to which I contributed more often. I've skimmed back the number of lists I subscribe to, but I still have a sense of community on the Internet, and it's largely a community I've created and nurtured myself. People who read The BradLands write to me to share links they think I might enjoy. Sometimes, things I mention in my weblog show up in other folks' weblogs too, with credit to me for pointing the way. Cameron Barrett has created the best of both worlds with his CamList,[18] a mailing list for readers of his weblog. My weblog is linked from several others, and theirs from mine. We are a community, of sorts, a small town sharing gossip and news, recreation and sport, laughter and tears, all for the commonweal. And, for the most part, we're friendly to strangers.

It's that last part that's distressing to some folks who've taken a step back and looked at the relatively young practice of weblogging. The tendency of identical or similar links to show up in several different logs, and the frequency of reciprocal links among webloggers is seen as perhaps unhealthy, a form of incest that—we're told—can lead to a flattened sameness among our pages.

I haven't seen anything approaching a day when all of the dozen or so weblogs I read daily have completely identical links. On the occasions when two or more of us point to the same stories, well, it's because those are the big stories on the 'net (or at least among geeks) that day. It's no different than those occasions when channels 2, 4, 5, 8 and 11 all lead with the same feature on the evening news.

In fact, in the offline world, that sort of thing is much more common. Our weblogs, by contrast, are incredible in their manifold diversity.

Those who would dismiss weblogging as a pointless self-referential exercise or, in vulgar parlance, a big ol' Internet-based circle jerk, aren't looking toward the future.

I am. Over the next few months, I'll be narrowing the focus of The BradLands somewhat, limiting the topics that are regularly noted in the weblog to those that most interest me. (How limiting this is remains to be seen; I have quite catholic interests.) But, with time, The BradLands will evolve with a unique voice, a definite attitude, a clearer motivation.

Meanwhile, other folks will be starting weblogs of their own, defined by their own interests, published with their own voices. As more and more do so, the weblog movement will begin to realize its true power, a more widely distributed version of what the Open Directory and other collaborative web directories have promised but only minimally delivered.

Hundreds of individuals, sorting through the Internet, pointing to the links that they find interesting and that they believe would interest their friends and colleagues and a few bystanders besides.

Sure, two or four or more of us will point to the same "big story" from time to time, or even to the same "small story." That's OK. I have a different set of readers than Laurel[19] does, and she attracts a different crowd than Cam,[20] and Jorn[21] has yet another audience. There's some overlap, but there's a whole lot of difference too, because we're different people.

An old maxim states that editors separate the wheat from the chaff and then publish the chaff.

As the weblog movement matures, our sites will wrest editorial authority from the few editors of today and divide it among the many. "They" can continue to publish the chaff; we'll be there to point our hungry readers toward the wheat. Hopefully, we'll have fun doing it and learn a lot along the way.

And that, my friends, is why I weblog.

PART TWO
Meet the Bloggers

7

We Didn't Start the Weblogs

Nikolai Nolan

TO THE TUNE OF BILLY JOEL'S "WE DIDN'T START THE FIRE"

Jeffrey Zeldman, Scripting News, OnFocus, MemePool,
Accidental, Wendell Wittler, Pith and Vinegar,
BluishOrange, Robot Wisdom, Windowseat, and Television,
MetaFilter, Yuppie Slayer, Whim and Vinegar

Slightly North, Strange Brew, Lake Effect, RandomFoo,
WebWaste, 2xy, RandomWalks, and Flutterby,
Calamondin, MetaScene, Ribbit, and MTHology,
David Gagne, Wockerjabby, Little Yellow Different[1]

We didn't start the weblogs
They were always thinking
Of good sites for linking
We didn't start the weblogs
No, we didn't incite 'em
But we're trying to write 'em

RiotHero, Medley, Chrish, Looka, Danelope, and Jish,
Hack the Planet, Mr. Barrett, Ethel the Blog,
Planet Jon, Donkeymon, Day 17, Gammatron,
/Usr/Bin/Girl, and SurvivorBlog,
MegNut, Kottke, Saturn, Weblog Wannabe,
Swallowing Tacks, Anthony, Thoughts at Random, Entropy,
Geegaw, EatonWeb, Caterina, EvHead,
LinkinLog, Openlog, Electric Biscuit[2]

We didn't start the weblogs
They were always thinking
Of good sites for linking
We didn't start the weblogs
No, we didn't incite 'em
But we're trying to write 'em

LOL, Webmistress, Mermaniac, Hit or Miss,
Geeknik, Blog by Night, Touched By an Impudite,
RasterWeb, Montreal, Craig is Periodical,
Psionic, Other Side, KarenH[3] is hard to rhyme
Uh-huh, uh-huh
Inessential, BradLands, Packet Monkeys, Mister Pants,
SixFoot6, Baylink, Not So Soft, and ThinkDink,
LarkFarm, PeterMe, Moronic and Apathy,
Mellifluous, Techno, Ctrl-Alt-Ego[4]

We didn't start the weblogs
They were always thinking
Of good sites for linking
We didn't start the weblogs
No, we didn't incite 'em
But we're trying to write 'em

Hemisphere, Swirlee, What's On It For Me,
Wetlog, BrainLog, NeoFlux, and Stuffed Dog,
Somnolent, Jauteria, Re-run, Netdyslexia,
Dan Says, CamWorld, PlasticBag, MetaGrrrl,
Harmful, Bits, and Q, Rebecca, and MetaCubed,
NTK, My Latte, Fiendish Thingy, and Array[5]

We didn't start the weblogs
They were always thinking
Of good sites for linking
We didn't start the weblogs
No, we didn't incite 'em
But we're trying to write 'em

ThinkHole, NeilAlien, Dack and Senior Citizen,
GeneHack, FastHack, Kestrel's Nest, Tomalak,
Bump, Harrumph, and Backup Brain, IRC on Wednesdays,
Andrew Abb is in Japan, Prol is in the Netherlands,
South by Southwest, stuff to buy, Power Bloggers, junior high,
Weblog rings, filter things, ads, cams, some can sing,
Blogger formats them for you, Manila and Pitas too,
Beebo ratings, blogger wars,[6] I[7] can't[8] link[9] them[10] anymore[11]

We didn't start the weblogs
They were always thinking
Of good sites for linking
We didn't start the weblogs
But when we are gone
Will they still blog on, and on, and on, and on, and on, and
on, and on, and on

We didn't start the weblogs
They were always thinking

Of good sites for linking
We didn't start the weblogs
No, we didn't incite 'em
But we're trying to write 'em

We didn't start the weblogs
They were always thinking
Of good sites for linking
We didn't start the weblogs
No, we didn't incite 'em
But we're trying to write 'em

'

You've Got Blog: How to Put Your Business, Your Boyfriend, and Your Life Online

Rebecca Mead
November 13, 2000

1

Meg Hourihan was in a bad mood. She had nothing major to worry about, but she was afflicted by the triple malaise of a woman in her late twenties: (a) the weather was lousy; (b) she was working too hard; and (c) she didn't have a boyfriend. Nothing, not even eating, seemed very interesting to her. The only thing that did sound appealing was moving to France and finding a hot new French boyfriend, but even when she talked about that idea she struck a sardonic, yeah-right-like-I'm-really-going-to-do-that kind of tone.

I know this about Meg because I read it a few months ago on her personal website, which is called megnut.com. I've been reading Megnut for a while now, and so I know all kinds of things about its author, like how much she loved Hilary Swank in "Boys Don't Cry," how she wishes there were good fish tacos to be had in San Francisco, and where she lives. I know she's a feminist, and that she writes short stories, and that she's close to her mom. I know that she's a little dreamy and idealistic; that she fervently believes there is a distinction between "dot-com people," who are involved in the Internet for its I.P.O. opportunities, and "Web people," who are in love with the imaginative possibilities presented by the medium, and that she counts herself among the latter.

Meg is one of the founders of a company called Pyra, which produces an Internet application known as Blogger. Blogger, which can be used free on the Internet, is a tool for creating a new kind of website that is known as a "weblog," or "blog," of which Megnut is an example. A blog consists primarily of links to other websites and commentary about those links. Having a blog is rather like publishing your own, online version of *Reader's Digest*, with daily updates: you troll the Internet, and, when you find an article or a website that grabs you, you link to it—or, in weblog parlance, you "blog" it. Then other people who have blogs—they are known as bloggers—read your blog, and if they like it they blog your blog on their own blog.

Blogs often consist of links to articles that readers might otherwise have missed, and thus make for informative reading: it was via an excellent blog called Rebecca's Pocket that I learned, for instance, that the Bangkok transit authority had introduced a ladies-only bus to protect female passengers from strap-hanging molestation. It also led me to a site devoted to burritos, where I underwent an online burrito analysis, in which my personality type was diagnosed according to my favorite burrito elements: "Your pairing of a meat-free burrito and all those fatty toppings indicates a dangerous ability to live with illusions." Blogs often include links to sites that illuminate the matter at hand. For example, when Meg wrote about planting a plumeria cutting, she linked to a site called the Plumeria Place, which included a picture and a description of the plant.

Many bloggers have Internet-related jobs, and so they use their sites to keep other bloggers informed of the latest news in the world of Web design or copyright law. Jason Kottke, a Web designer from Minneapolis who maintains a site called kottke.org, is widely admired among bloggers as a thoughtful critic of Web culture. (On the strength of the picture transmitted by his Webcam, he is also widely perceived as very cute. If you read around among blogs, you find that Kottke is virtually beset by blogging groupies.) Getting blogged by Kottke, or by Meg Hourihan or one of her colleagues at Pyra, is the blog equivalent of having your book featured on "Oprah": it generally means a substantial boost in traffic, enough, perhaps, to earn the blog a mention on beebo.org, which has functioned as a blog best-seller list. (An example from a blog called fairvue.com: "Jason K. linked to Fairvue. My life is now complete.")

The weblog format of links and commentary has been around for some years, but in the early days of weblogging the sites had to be built by hand, one block of code at a time, which meant that they were produced only by a handful of technology mavens. There were a few weblogs that earned a following among nontech civilians—Jim Romenesko's Medianews, a weblog of stories about the media business, is one; Arts & Letters Daily, a digest of intellectual affairs, is another—but most remained more specialized. A year and a half ago, there were only fifty or so weblogs; now the number has increased to thousands, with blogs like Megnut getting around a thousand visits a day. This growth is due in large part to Blogger, and a couple of other weblogging tools such as Pitas and Editthispage, which have made launching a personal website far simpler.

Most of the new blogs are, like Megnut, intimate narratives rather than digests of links and commentary; to read them is to enter a world in which the personal lives of participants have become part of the public domain. Because the main audience for blogs is other bloggers, blogging etiquette requires that, if someone blogs your blog, you blog his blog back. Reading blogs can feel a lot like listening in on a conversation among a group of friends who all know each other really well. Blogging, it turns out, is the CB radio of the Dave Eggers generation. And that is how, when Meg Hourihan followed up her French-boyfriend-depression posting with a stream-of-consciousness blog entry a few weeks later saying that she had developed a crush on someone but was afraid to act on it—"Maybe I've become very good at eluding love, but that's not a complaint, I just want to get it all out of my head and put it somewhere else," she wrote—her love life became not just her business but the business of bloggers everywhere.

2

Pyra, the company that produces Blogger, has its offices on the ground floor of a warehouse building on Townsend Street in SoMa, the former industrial district that is now home to many of San Francisco's Internet businesses. The company, which was founded last year by Evan Williams (who has his own blog, evhead.com) in collaboration with Meg Hourihan, occupies two computer-filled rooms that face each other across an atrium littered with random pieces of office furniture discarded by Internet startups whose fortunes took a dive when the Nasdaq did, last April. Pyra survived the dive, with some help from venture capitalists, and from Mr. and Mrs. Hourihan, Meg's parents. (More recently, Advance Publications, which publishes the *New Yorker*, invested in Pyra.) Still, Ev and Meg ruefully talk about how they managed to get through the summer of 1999, the season of implausible I.P.O.s, without becoming rich.

"We first met at a party," Meg explained, as she and I sat on a battered couch. Ev rolled his desk chair over to join us. Meg, who grew up in Boston and graduated from Tufts with a degree in English, is voluble and given to gesticulation. She is tall and athletic-looking, and has cropped spiky hair that last spring she bleached white-blond after polling the readers of her blog about her hairstyling options. Meg and Ev dated for a while before deciding that their shared passion for the Internet did not translate into a shared passion for each other; but then Ev drafted Meg to help him start Pyra, the goal of which was to develop a Web-based tool that would help project managers share information with co-workers. (They have since been joined by four other friends.)

"I knew she was very good at helping me think about ideas," Ev said. Ev comes from Nebraska. He once blogged an aerial photograph of the family farm and is taciturn and ironic; he has a beetling brow and a Tintin coif. In 1991, he dropped out of the University of Nebraska–Lincoln after a year and launched his first Internet company, for which he still owes his parents money.

Blogger wasn't part of Pyra's original plan; Ev and a colleague, Paul Bausch, built it for fun, and then launched it on the Web one week in the summer of 1999, when Meg was on vacation. That fall, Blogger found plenty of users among geeks who were glad to have a tool that made weblogging easier; only recently, though, did Ev and Meg set aside their other Pyra plans. "It took us a long time to realize what we had with Blogger," Meg said.

That afternoon, Meg sat down with me at her computer—I tried to stay out of the range of the Webcam that is trained on her whenever she sits at her desk—and showed me how Blogger works. To use Blogger, it helps to know a little of the computer language html, but, once you've set up your site, adding new chunks of text is as easy as sending an email. Meg clicked open the Blogger inputting box, typed a few words, and showed me how she could hit one button and send the text to her site. The creators of Blogger think it may make posting items on the Web a little too easy; a new term, "blogorrhea," has been coined to de-scribe the kind of entries—"I'm tired" or "This sucks"—that are the work of the unimaginative blogger.

While I was sitting at Meg's desk, I noticed the bookmarks that she had on her Web browser. Among them were evhead.com and kottke.org. She had also marked Jason Kottke's Webcam. Jason Kottke was the object of the crush that Meg had described in her blog a few months earlier. They met last March, at South by Southwest, an alternative-culture conference that takes place in Austin every spring.

"I recognized him immediately," Meg wrote in an email to me. "He was taller than I thought he'd be, but I knew it was him." She had been reading his blog, kottke.org, for ages. "I always thought he seemed cool and intelligent . . . but I thought he was a bit conceited. He was so well-known, and he wrote once about tak-ing some online I.Q. tests and he actually posted his results, which I thought was showoffish."

After meeting Jason, Meg changed her mind: "He seemed not at all conceited like I thought, and actually pretty funny and nice, and cute, much cuter than he ever appeared on his Webcam."

Meg made sure she had an excuse to stay in touch. She offered to send Jason a customized version of Blogger code for him to try on kottke.org. Once she got back to San Francisco, she said, "I wrote on Megnut that I had a crush, and he emailed me and said, 'Who's the crush on? Spill it, sister.' So I emailed him back and said it was him. He was really surprised." Meg took further elec-tronic action to advance her aims, and altered her website so that it included her ICQ number—the number someone would need to send her an instant message, even though the last thing she wanted was to be inundated with instant messages from strangers. A couple of days later, Jason ICQ'd her for the first time. ("He fell for my trick," she said.) That night, they instant-messaged for three hours. A week later, she shifted technologies again, and called him on the telephone. Then she invited him to San Francisco, and that was that.

Meg and Jason had been dating for two months when I visited San Francisco, and he was due to arrive from Minneapolis for the weekend. Meg told me about a Web device she uses called Flight Tracker: you type in a flight number, and a map is displayed, with an icon representing the location of the airplane. "I always look at it and think, Oh, he's over Nebraska now," she said.

I already knew that Meg and Jason were involved because I'd been reading their websites; although neither of them had written anything about the relationship, there were hints throughout their recent entries. Those hints had also been under discussion on a website called MetaFilter. MetaFilter is a "community weblog," which means that anyone who is a member can post a link to it. Most of the posts to MetaFilter are links to news stories or weird websites, but in early June someone named Monkeyboy had linked to a photograph of Meg and Jason looking into Jason's bathroom mirror. The picture was posted on a website belonging to a friend of Meg's who collects photographs of the mirrors of Web celebrities. Monkeyboy also linked to Megnut's "crush" entry, and to an entry that Jason had written on kottke.org about Meg's site design, and he posted them all on MetaFilter with the words "So what's up with this? I think there's something going on here." This generated a lively discussion, with some bloggers furthering the gossip by linking to other blogs whose authors had confessed to having crushes on Jason, while others wrote in suggesting it was none of anyone's business.

When I looked back at Jason's blog for the period just after he met Meg, I found no references to a romance. Jason's style is a little more sober. But there was one entry in which he seemed to be examining the boundary between his Web life and his non-Web life. He'd written that there were things going on in his life that were more personal than the stuff he usually wrote about in his weblog. "Why don't I just write it down somewhere private . . . a Word doc on my computer or in a paper diary?" he asked himself, and his readers. "Somehow, that seems strange to me though. . . . The Web is the place for you to express your thoughts and feelings and such. To put those things elsewhere seems absurd."

One day, I met Meg and Jason for breakfast. Jason, who is twenty-seven, tall, with short hair and sideburns, was wearing jeans and a "Princess Mononoke" T-shirt. She ordered a tofu scramble and soy latte, he had real eggs. I asked what it was like to have their private lives discussed among the members of their virtual community, and they said they thought it was funny. I asked whether they ever included hidden messages to each other in their blogs, an idea that seemed to surprise them. "Well, I did once use that word 'tingly,'" Meg said. Jason blushed.

A few days later, they stoked the gossip further by posting identical entries on their websites: word-for-word accounts of seeing a young girl on a bicycle in the street, and descriptions of the childhood memories that it triggered. Then a strange thing happened. One by one, several bloggers copied the little-girl entry into their blogs, as if they had seen the child on the bicycle, too. Other bloggers started to write parodies of the little-girl entry. Still other bloggers started to post messages to MetaFilter, asking what the hell was going on with all these sightings of little girls. When I sent Meg an email about this outbreak, she wrote back, "I was especially struck by the number of people who thought it was a big prank pulled by the 'popular' kids to make fun of the uncool kids."

3

There have been some ostentatious retreats from the blogging frenzy: last June, one well-known blogger named Derek Powazek announced in his blog that he wanted no part of it anymore, and that instead of addressing himself to the blogger community at large he would henceforth be writing with only a few friends and family members in mind. This announcement provoked a flurry of postings from neophyte bloggers, who feared they were facing the Twilight of Blogging before they had really had a chance to enjoy the Dawn of Blogging.

The people at Pyra, having generated a blog explosion with their Blogger software, aren't entirely happy about the way blogs have developed. "It's like being frustrated with your kid, when you know he could be doing so much more," Ev told me. He and Meg have been developing different uses for Blogger, including ones from which they might actually make some money. One idea is to install Blogger on the intranets of companies, so that it can be used as a means of letting large groups share information. (Cisco is currently experimenting with using Blogger in-house to keep minutes of project meetings up to date.)

Meanwhile, Meg and Ev have developed a whole new level of celebrity status. Not long ago, a group of bloggers created a community blog called The Pyra Shrine. There are posts about how hot Meg is ("Megnut is da bomb. She's one kewl lady") and whether Ev needs a personal assistant ("You know, to make him coffee and get him stuff. I'd do it. For free, even!"). The whole thing is very silly, and completely irresistible if you're a reader of Megnut or Evhead, or, indeed, if you are the creator of Megnut or Evhead. Meg linked to it on her site recently, and wrote, "O.K., I have to admit, this The Pyra Shrine cracks me up."

It was through The Pyra Shrine that I learned, one day last month, that Jason was moving to San Francisco. ("That's a big sacrifice. He must really love her," one of the Shrine contributors had posted.) I emailed Meg, who told me that Jason had taken a new Web design job and was driving across the country; he was probably in Wyoming at that very moment. I remarked that since he was in a car she couldn't use Flight Tracker to see where he was.

"Oh yeah, it's so bad," she wrote back. "I'm so used to being able to communicate with him, or at least check in in some way all the time (Webcam, Flight Tracker, ICQ, email, etc.) and now there's nothing. Well, except for phone at night, but still, seems like nothing compared with what I've gotten used to."

Later that night, I called Meg, and she sounded excited. "He should be here in three or four days," she said. Having mastered the techniques for having a digital relationship, she was finally ready for an analog one; and she hadn't even had to move to France to get it.

9

Deconstructing "You've Got Blog"

Joe Clark
January 25, 2002

IT'S A FIXTURE OF LIFE, AS THE 21ST CENTURY BEGINS ITS SLOW download into history, that media can and do refer to and build atop themselves, adding layers of remove from the source or original subject. Here's a Canadian example: Bruce McDonald's film *Hard Core Logo* (1996) was adapted as a screenplay by Noel Baker from a 1993 book of doggerel by Michael Turner, later to be adapted *into* a comic book by Nick Craine (1997) while Baker wrote *Hard Core Roadshow* (1997), a non-fiction book on making the movie.

How's that for meta?

My contribution to this collection conforms to that trend, straddling a pair of distinct media: "Deconstructing 'You've Got Blog,'" as you read it here, is an adaptation of a webpage (a "posting," really, from November 2000) that analyzed a magazine article about websites.

I've done a lot of writing for the print medium as a journalist for magazines and newspapers; I've also written a book and a handful of scripts. I've been online since 1991 (look me up via a Google Groups search if you like), and I've written over 500 items for my own websites. I maintain four different weblogs (links to which are found at joeclark.org/weblogs/). But before working on this adaptation, it had never occurred to me how profoundly the qualities of the eventual medium shape one's manner of expression.

The original posting used HTML structures like tables for a columnar layout and ordered and unordered lists ([ol][/ol] and [ul][/ul]) and block quotations ([blockquote][/blockquote]) to organize topics. It may be a shibboleth for novice Web authors to use built-in formats like lists (because, we are told by advisors who are themselves bad writers in the first place, people *scan* webpages rather than read them), but I tend to view HTML structures as merely tools in one's armamentarium, to be used or ignored at will. Yet since I opted for the path of HTML structure at the outset, what alterations are necessary to make the same piece *work* in a printed book?

Damned if I know. Even self-medication with the strongest drug I take, the double long espresso, failed to unleash an alternative from the recesses of my mind. It looks like you, dear reader, are stuck with a weblike and decidedly untypographic amalgam of bullets and nested indention. I expect this may end up feeling as forced and ill-advised as aiming a camcorder at a high-school play and calling it a feature film. You have my apologies in advance. But look on the bright side: the literary theorists stand to gain a whole new domain for masters' theses in *problematizing the Web/print literary interface*. Just be sure to give me a nice plug.

Our Story Begins

"You've Got Blog," Rebecca Mead's trenchant analysis of the blog-abetted romance of Jason Kottke and Meg Hourihan, finally put us weblogger kidz on the map big-time. The article is excellent, full stop. Mead accurately, fairly, and indeed winsomely encapsulates the blogging phenomenon through the tried-and-true narrative device of personifying an abstract process with a hero (and heroine). In fact, Mead got so many things right that the story works on multiple levels; the knowing reader can identify a few truths a blogging neophyte could not. Let's explore, shall we?

1. *The unbearable incestuousness of blogging:* "The other people who have blogs . . . read your blog, and if they like it they blog your blog on their own blog."

- The *nominal* purpose of weblogs is to point out links of interest that you, the reader, would not have run across yourself. A variant is the diaristic or daily-journal weblog.
- But since so many leading weblogs are written by folks in the Internet biz, their entire lives *are* online. You can write up what you did with your real-life friend yesterday, but you can't link to that experience. You *can* link to what your online friend *blogged* yesterday. The annotated-list-of-links weblog form, then, becomes one and the same with the diaristic form for webloggers in the Internet demimonde: links *are* diaries because life *is* the Web.
- This practice, however, defeats the original purpose of link-based weblogging—to find fresh new items online. It also defeats the purpose of the daily-journal blogging style, which lets perfect strangers peer into the fascinating or mundane lives of others, details they could not possibly know about by different means. Counterblogging fails the test of novelty two ways: the links aren't fresh (they've been traded back and forth like saliva in a kiss) and no new events from bloggers' real lives are depicted.

2. *The A-List:* "Jason Kottke . . . is widely admired among bloggers as a thoughtful critic of Web culture. . . . Getting blogged by

Kottke, or by Meg Hourihan or one of her colleagues at Pyra, is the blog equivalent of having your book featured on *Oprah*."

- Finally, independent confirmation of an obvious fact that is self-servingly denied by the weblog aristocracy itself: despite no appreciable difference in the "thoughtfulness" of their respective Web criticism, some webloggers are superstars.
- The myth, of course, holds that all bloggers are equal, because we all can set out our wares on the great egalitarian Internet, where the best ideas bubble to the surface. This free-market theory of information has superficial appeal, but reality is rather different.
- Jason's commentary is quite good (Meg's less so), but so is the commentary written by literally a dozen other bloggers I read, none of whom can create a miniature Slashdot effect by mentioning you. (I'm not citing any other bloggers here, by the way, whatever their fame or acumen. I'm limiting the name-dropping to the bloggers Rebecca Mead introduced into the discourse.)
- Jason's fame cannot be attributed solely to his cuteness (mentioned by Mead). I can think of a host of other A-list bloggers who are better-looking, not to mention having a bit more meat on the bones, and I am aware that there are a lot of attractive bloggeuses. Moreover, one A-list blogger is spectacularly ugly, but that has not impeded his star status.
- Web-design skills cannot account for everything, either. Jason's site, in its various forms, offers a middling level of programming complexity. Yet I can name three other A-list bloggers, and a far greater number digging for coal with their bare hands in the caverns of the Net, whose sites are more complex and better looking.

- A small number of A-list bloggers run weblogs that are effectively *undesigned*, a positioning statement that aims to showcase their ideas more prominently, but their ideas aren't markedly superior to other bloggers' in the first place.
- Any way you cut it, there is no rational or even pseudo-rational explanation for the distribution of fame in the blog biz. I suppose fame is like that sometimes.

3. *Publicity stunt:* I recall the topic of the relentlessly counterblogged "memory" of a young girl riding her bicycle. An entry along these lines appeared in dozens of blogs:

A little girl rides her bike up my street, streamers flapping from the handlebars, a cheerful basket fastened up front. As I get out of my car and start up the steps of the house, she waves and calls out "Hi, Mr. Cooley!" I pause on the steps and wave back as she continues down the block. She'll make two or three more circles of the wide, grassy parkway that separates the north and south sides of our street and then, I imagine, go home for supper.

This happens at least once a week, and has gone on for much of the summer.

My name, incidentally, is not Cooley, but she thinks it is. Ours is a neighborhood where most of the houses are at least a century old and are referred to by the names of their original owners or the most recent residents of long standing. The Parks House. The Chouteau House, across the street. We have lived here only eight years, so ours is still the Cooley House. We won't get naming rights for another decade at the inside.

The little girl has probably heard her parents or grandparents describe my home as the Cooley House, pointing it out on walks on sultry summer evenings before the sun slips leisurely behind the Arch and the city air begins to cool. With perfect logic, she assumes that because I live in the Cooley House, I must be Mr. Cooley.

I do not know her name, but tonight, as the little girl excitedly pedals away, I wave and call to her back, "Hi, Sarah! Be careful, now!"

She will be Sarah because the girl on the bike in my neighborhood when I was growing up was Sarah. She won't get to be Britney or Courteney or Tiffany for another decade at the inside.

(That was Brad Graham's version from bradlands.com. I fixed its misspellings and malapropisms.) In response to this promiscuous counterblogging, Rebecca Mead quotes Meg Hourihan: "I was especially struck by the number of people who thought it was a big prank pulled by the 'popular' kids to make fun of the uncool kids." That clearly was not the intent, but the effect was the same, highlighting the incestuousness and insularity of the crème-de-la-blogging-crème.

- This raises the issue of in-jokes. Mead broadly implies that Meg and Jason were using their blogs to send coded messages to one another—ofttimes subconsciously. Very astute outside observers were able to put two and two together and infer that some kind of love was blossoming between the blogging dynamic duo. (The observers wouldn't have gone to that trouble were Jason and Meg not A-list bloggers whose sites were scoured daily.)
- The girl-on-a-bike prank was the rankest example yet of the mutual admiration society of the weblog intelligentsia, deploying multiple identical coded messages—*false* memories of a little girl on a bicycle, duplicated by copy and paste, and not always even read all the way through[1] (as Tom Coates of plasticbag.org admitted; Cf. those mis-

spellings and malapropisms)—merely because they *could* do it.

- The counterblogging form pretends to function as a conversation, but, unlike email or instant messaging or any kind of threaded discussion forum, the effect is one of talking at people rather than *with* them. But you're talking at them in public, rather like chatting on a cellphone at the mall, only in this case third parties stand a good chance of reading both sides of the conversation.

4. *The Golden Age:* Derek Powazek's retrenchment[2] from blogging "provoked a flurry of postings from neophyte bloggers, who feared they were facing the Twilight of Blogging before they had really had a chance to enjoy the Dawn of Blogging." Setting aside for the moment that Powazek has been well and ably back in the blogging game since December 2000, this entire question revolves around a single word: *audience.*

- It is idealistic in the extreme to counsel bloggers not to concern themselves with an audience. The advice "Write for yourself," while appropriate for a self-help course, applies poorly to the Web. Before the Internet, you could write all you wanted, but unless you had actual talent and enough persuasiveness to win over an editor, your work would go unpublished, and only you would ever read it.
- Now, according to the egalitarian mythos of the Web, anyone can publish. You skip the step of requiring an editor and publisher, but no one is willing to skip the step of requiring an audience. Take it from someone who wrote since age seven: few are the writers who do it for themselves. Even handwritten diaries will be discovered posthumously, as every diarist knows deep down.

- These "neophyte" bloggers happen upon one of the automated weblogging tools and discover with delight that another barrier has fallen—the need to learn HTML. And they see what the A-list kids are doing: the neophytes read all the preëminent weblogs. (How could they miss 'em? They lead the "Other blogs" columns on hundreds of sites.)

- Quickly the culture of upward mobility is inculcated: *if Jason Kottke can be famous and well-loved—living in Minnesota, for gosh sakes!—I can, too. Can't I?*

- When a very-big-name blogger like Derek Powazek partially renounces the medium, to the neophyte blogger it's like packing up and moving to hip, hot, sexy Prague only to find out it was a happening place two years ago, having taken that long for the happeningness to gain the attention of leading style magazines.

- The fears of these neophyte bloggers are, in fact, entirely valid, but may require restatement. It's not that you missed the Golden Age. It's just that the age is golden only for others. And there is pretty much no way to breach the velvet rope: if you're not an A-list blogger, you will stay off that list forever. Note that you can't even really "marry into money," as was possible in the olden days. Stars cavort with other stars, even in the most extreme cases: Elizabeth Taylor married actors twice as often as truckers.[3] Jason Kottke moved across the United States for love of Meg Hourihan (they live together in San Francisco), not for an unsung woman who doesn't even use a computer.

- The desire for approval is natural and human and should not elicit scorn. The desire for *recognition* is even more primal ("I exist. Talk to me") and is to be encouraged. Yet weblogging raises false hopes for both.

- *Recognition*, in this case, is a synonym for *audience*, and, in the time-honoured tradition of starstruck social-climbers, the A-list bloggers are the ones with the biggest audiences, and everybody wants to be like them.

- What the huddled masses yearning to blog their way into superstardom are left with, then, is not merely talking at people, but talking at a perennially minuscule group of people. It's a source of frustration: it shatters the illusions of communication and dialogue, a shadow of which we notice when the A-list blithely blogs and counterblogs itself. The thinking is: "they get to have a semblance of a conversation [however illusory; see above], so why can't we?"

"Yeah? So?"

Of course, if you are not actually predisposed to buy any of the foregoing, everything I have written so far may seem like unreconstructed whining. In fact, other bloggers described the posting thus:

"Somewhat self-important"—Dan Hartung

"A steaming pile of crap"—Tom Coates

"'Grapes' . . . 'sour'"—Jason Kottke

"Just another lame ploy by a known hitslut"—Rebekah Jude Allen

(Here's what Rebecca Mead had to say: "This seems to me to be very astute." So, I mean, *you* tell *me*.)

In the *New Yorker*, Rebecca Mead quotes Jason Kottke: "He'd written that there were things going on in his life that were more personal than the stuff he usually wrote about in his weblog. 'Why don't I just write it down somewhere private . . . a Word doc on my computer or in a paper diary?' he asked himself and his readers. 'Somehow, that seems strange to me, though. . . . The Web is the place for you to express your thoughts and feelings and such. To put those things elsewhere seems absurd.'" In keeping with the practice of documenting deep-seated feelings and experiences in plain public view, it's time to explain why I wrote this companion piece.

You may think I'm jealous. Trust me, I'm not. Mildly envious, yes, but not jealous.

I wrote the original posting while working as an "office lady" ("OL"), to use the quaint Japanese locution. At age 35, I was a glorified secretary—a pink-collar profession where my genuinely vast software knowledge, impeccable writing skills, and 90-words-a-minute typing were useful, if not highly remunerated. In a particularly unchallenging assignment, I knew I had maybe three hours of actual work to finish in the run of a day; I was, moreover, unsupervised in my own veal-fattening pen, and everyone expected me to be typing away all day. I even had a copyholder, all the better to read the original Rebecca Mead article and engage in surgical-quality rhetorical curettage.

I was, at this point, not only a qualified writer-editor but a struggling "content consultant." I started a fledgling content consultancy, named contenu.nu ("content" in French, plus the memorable reduplicative .nu domain, which the island of Niue has sold on the open market for years), with a few of my friends as allies, if not actual business partners. But they all had day jobs (mostly in the Web field), while all I had to show at contenu.nu was my kvetchy weblog on online content, the NUblog, widely unread though maintained to this very day. I was barely making a living as an OL and was a failure at rounding up "content" business. Even OLing was sporadic, leaving me with extensive high-stress "free" time in which to pound out kvetchy content ruminations at 90 words a minute.

But *all my friends*, I reiterate, *had day jobs*, as did seemingly every-one else who ran a blog. The straw that broke this camel's back was the knowledge that A-list bloggers, and many of those unlucky enough not to be on that list, led well-funded and more-or-less-rewarding lives in the Internet industry. How many times did we run across a blog posting like this hypothetical composite example?

> Rio just came out with a new MP3 player shaped like a walnut— and about the same size. They say it'll sync with my Palm, which is too damn new for me to have synced it with my old Palm, let alone the Cube or the PowerBook. Anyway, something to pick up after Saturday brunch with the blog crew. Maybe I should retire my iPod. . . .

I'd be less inclined to complain if I'd been able to share in the Internet bounty in even the most trivial way. None of us weblog-gers is particularly wealthy; few of us became dot-com million-aires. It's just that everyone but me got to make a living. It bugged me that the A-list kids were not really any smarter, or any better at Web design, or had anything particularly better to say than so many of the plebes. Their fame is inexplicable, but fa-mous they were and are—*and* they were able to keep their heads above water. It's that combination I resented.

Elizabeth Taylor was at least beautiful and could act, when not knocking back the sauce and buying diamonds by the barrel. What enabled an anointed cadre of objectively undifferentiable webloggers to be viewed as demigods escapes me. And it does in fact chafe against my egalitarian instincts. Many of us are as good as they are. (There. I put myself in one of the camps. And not the one that elicits profiles in the *New Yorker*.)

It is no longer fair to say, as my original posting did, that "we can look forward to further triumphs and prosperity for Jason,

Meg, Derek, and the other quarterbacks and cheerleaders of Weblog High. Successful people remain successful." Meg Hourihan was forced to go freelance (a euphemism that rivals "denies wrongdoing" and "left to pursue other interests") after her employer Pyra, inventor of the mighty Blogger application, was driven into a snowbank by mismanagement. But she's the exception: A-list bloggers have, in general, remained on the A-list *and* remained employed. And besides, doesn't she have a boyfriend who enjoys continued adulation *and* a good job?

If I'd been able to get a piece of that action when I originally wrote the piece, I'd have been right in there rootin' the A-list on. I'm a journalist; *of course* I approve of worthy people getting good press. The origin of this deconstruction, then, is a form of economic resentment. And if you think I make this admission lightly, especially in a book that may still be around in 20 years, you underestimate how I felt about being poor at the time. Really, my feelings have not changed even as my lot in life has improved. I never managed to land a Web job, but I wrote a book—*Building Accessible Websites*, on Web accessibility—and started doing accessibility consulting. I hope that, at some future time, a duo comprised of an economist and an anthropologist will write a history of the employment jungle that was the Internet "bubble."

A blog is a form of exteriorized psychology. It's a part of you, or of your psyche; while a titanium hip joint or a pacemaker might bring technology *inside* the corporeal you, a weblog uses technology to bring the psychological you *outside* of it. Your weblog acts as a new limb, a new mouth, and a new hemisphere of the brain. Once those new organs come into being, you're no more likely to remove or amputate them than the original organic equipment they augment. I continue to write weblogs—not for money, not for renown, not for anyone but myself.

10

Portrait of the Blogger as a Young Man

Julian Dibbell

The ascendance of the search engine has done nothing to stem the tide of the Web's original filter: the personal weblog. Julian Dibbell gets inside the obsessions of one of the Net's most prolific bloggers.

JORN BARGER IS A COLLECTOR, OF A SORT—THOUGH YOU WOULDN'T know what sort, exactly, from gazing on his worldly possessions. A long-haired, thick-bearded former artificial-intelligence (AI) programmer in his forties, Barger lives in genteel poverty, sharing an apartment with roommates in Chicago's scruffy West Rogers Park neighborhood. His bedroom once held a lot of books, but he had to sell them off some time ago; the principal fixtures remaining are a secondhand Macintosh with built-in television, a boom-box radio, and a bed. Barger spends his days in the bed, and there—sitting with the Mac's keyboard in his lap and its monitor beside him—he collects: A color-coded map of the world's language families. A discussion of the various titles Proust considered and discarded for *Remembrance of Things Past*. A *National Enquirer* article on "who's doing yoga in Hollywood." A

BBC item on the evolution of cooperation among capuchin monkeys. Some photos of Fisher-Price Little People repainted as characters from *Futurama*. A FAIR analysis of recent mainstream news coverage of the IMF and the World Bank. An oddly evocative Webcam shot from the Jennicam website. A tribute to the Spanish-language children's television show *El Club de los Tigritos*. A compilation of Noam Chomsky resources on the Web. A detailed list of textual correspondences between James Joyce's *Ulysses* and Homer's *Odyssey*. A phrase that Barger dreamed last night on the edge of waking.

All these items—and many, many more—have been collected over the years as links on Barger's website, Robot Wisdom.[1] His collection is what's known these days as a weblog, or, to its friends, a "blog"—a regularly updated site containing links to pages the author finds interesting, typically with commentary attached. Barger coined the term himself when he started his weblog in 1997, though he was hardly the first person to have kept one. For as long as there have been browsers, there have been surfers gathering and sharing their favorite finds. The father of browsers himself—Mosaic author Marc Andreessen—is sometimes cited as the founding blogger, for the seminal What's New page he maintained in the early days of the Web.

But weblogs have come a long way since then, and Barger—well, Barger has plainly taken the concept to another level altogether. The word "obsession" comes to mind, though "passion," I suppose, is a kinder and maybe fairer name for what drives him to blog. He derives no revenues from the Robot Wisdom site; there are no advertisements on it, banner or otherwise. There are hardly any graphics at all, in fact. Just links—miles and miles of them, discerningly selected, pithily annotated, stacked one on top of another all the way down the main page and off into years' worth of monthly archives.

During the first two years of Robot Wisdom, the weblog was Barger's full-time occupation. Full time: he sat in bed surfing and linking all day long and had, he says, no job to support the habit. Last August, he finally cut back on the logging, limiting it to just a couple hours a day, but only so that he could devote more time to other aspects of the site. He spends the better part of his days working on long-term projects that surround and extend the daily log—link-studded FAQs on various subjects (artificial intelligence, ASCII art, weblogs), Web-resource pages on his favorite artists and authors (Robert Stone, Thomas Pynchon, Joni Mitchell, the Incredible String Band), and above all his magnum opus: a vast hyperlinked and open-ended annotation of Joyce's *Ulysses* and *Finnegans Wake*.

His Joyce pages appear to be getting as popular with scholars as his weblog has long been with journalists, but Barger remains a dedicated amateur in both fields, intent on dodging the temptation to professionalize. He has not had good experiences with the traditional workplace. He gets by, he says, with odd bits of contract work (programming, the occasional Joyce article), with loans, and with economies. Serious economies.

"I live on bread and water," Barger explains. "So as not to submit to the Idiots."

Well, homemade vegetarian pizza and cheap, supermarket-brand coffee, actually.

But still.

What Is a Weblog, Really?

The question has taken on some urgency in the last year or so. In the beginning, it wasn't much of an issue. The earliest weblogs, from the What's New era, looked distinctly like stop-gap measures, after all—ad-hoc, interim attempts to organize the Web's

burgeoning chaos of attractions, serviceable at best until something more efficient came along. And when something more efficient did come along, in the form of search engines and hierarchical indexes, it seemed safe to assume that weblogs would
politely shrivel up and blow away.

Instead, though, they evolved, gradually feeling their way toward an unexpected maturity as a form. By now, hundreds of more
and less artfully maintained blogs have emerged—Lemonyellow,[2]
Boing Boing,[3] and Cardhouse[4] being just a few of the more memorable. There are specialty blogs, their links dedicated to music,[5]
or Web design,[6] or Jewishness.[7] A loosely collegial, cross-linking
community of webloggers has coalesced, trading advice, feedback,
and support. Software, like the increasingly popular Blogger,[8] is
being built to ease the tedious job of daily adding links.

And inevitably, money has begun to nibble at the edges of the
phenomenon. Master blogger Jim Romenesko has been hired by
the Poynter Foundation to maintain his heavily trafficked media-
gossip weblog full time; corporations have been rumored to set up
in-house intranet blogs to track potential markets and competitors;
and arguably, sites like About.com, laced with linky content driz-
zled out by semi-amateur specialists, have incorporated elements
of weblogging into their business models. Also inevitably, articles
have been written—in *Salon,* the *New York Times, Wired*—conse-
crating weblogs as yet another New New Thing: At one time or
another in the last 12 months, they have been the future of journalism, a budding branch on the tree of literature, or both.

In fact, they are neither, say some members of the Web's weary
anti-hype brigades. "Sorry, buddy—you're just a dork who can't
come up with anything more than a paragraph or two to say
every day," wrote *Teeth* e-zine's Ben Brown in an open letter to
webloggers last spring. "You're not a designer, you're not a writer,
and you're not an editor!"

Well, no, blogger, you're not. And therein lies your gift. Because even if it's true, the vast majority of blogs would not be missed by more than a handful of people were the earth to open up and swallow them, and even if the best are still no substitute for the sustained attention of literary or journalistic works, it's also true that sustained attention is not what weblogs are about anyway. At their most interesting they embody something that exceeds attention, and transforms it: they are constructed from and pay implicit tribute to a peculiarly contemporary sort of wonder.

A weblog really, then, is a *Wunderkammer*. That is to say, the genealogy of weblogs points not to the world of letters but to the early history of museums—to the "cabinet of wonders," or *Wunderkammer*, that marked the scientific landscape of Renaissance modernity: a random collection of strange, compelling objects, typically compiled and owned by a learned, well-off gentleman. A set of ostrich feathers, a few rare shells, a South Pacific coral carving, a mummified mermaid—the *Wunderkammer* mingled fact and legend promiscuously, reflecting European civilization's dazed and wondering attempts to assimilate the glut of physical data that science and exploration were then unleashing.

Just so, the weblog reflects our own attempts to assimilate the glut of immaterial data loosed upon us by the "discovery" of the networked world. And there are surely lessons for us in the parallel. For just as the cabinet of wonders took centuries to evolve into the more orderly, logically crystalline museum, so it may be a while before the chaos of the Web submits to any very tidy scheme of organization. If we hoped once to pass immediately from the Web's *Wunderkammer* era to its museum age—to fly without a hitch from *What's New* to *Yahoo!*—these days we're obliged to recognize that indexes and search engines are themselves barely adequate to the job of taming the data storm, that grows far faster than their ability to filter it. We remain in a kind of stupor before the Web's abundance, and we seem likely to stay in it indefinitely. We might as well learn how to live there.

We might also consider enjoying it while it lasts. After all, the passage from *Wunderkammer* to museum may have been a triumph for Western science, but it was a mixed bag for the Western soul. Wonder isn't easily replaced once mastery disperses it, and we may sorely miss our wonder at the Web if and when the wonder goes. Better we should savor it now—and what better form to savor it in than in its purest distillation on the Web, the blog?

(I should add, by the way, that I'm not the first person to draw the parallel between the weblog and the *Wunderkammer*. I should also add that I have no idea who was. I saw the connection made briefly, in passing, on a weblog somewhere amid my surfing, but I can't recall for the life of me which weblog it was. The finest search engines couldn't find it again for me, and neither could two other bloggers I asked, both of whom remembered seeing the remark but neither of whom could recollect where. It's out there somewhere, lost in the excess of the Web, as legendary now as any mermaid.)

One isn't born a blogger, surely, and yet in Jorn Barger's case one has to wonder. Decades before there was a Web, he was chasing links through thickets of loosely interconnected data and ideas.

"In 1970, I decided that what I wanted to do with my life was to try to find a way to do psychology scientifically," says Barger. "I wanted to find a way to have it be both good science and good spiritual ethics, and through the seventies I pursued that in various ways. By the end of the seventies, I'd come up with the idea of robot wisdom."

Robot wisdom? That's as good an encapsulation as any, and none are very good. Barger's ideas are at once subtle and florid, and they don't summarize easily. Suffice it to say that they're as much literary as scientific, and that they orbit a complicated connection between artificial intelligence and the masterworks of James Joyce. Barger discovered that link in the midst of trying to map out a programmable taxonomy of human emotions: "I started compiling index cards with little descriptions of human behavior, mostly taken from literature. And when I organized them I started seeing cyclical patterns emerging, and it reminded me of things I'd read long ago about Joyce. I discovered there were very close matches, and that Joyce was also trying to build this large-scale model of human psychology."

When Barger discovered the Net in the late eighties, he threw his ideas at it with all the energy of an author finding his first audience. He became a netnews junkie, posting wit and wisdom to newsgroups from comp.ai to rec.arts.ascii-art to alt.music.alternative.female. He got into flamewars, deeply, some of them going "thermonuclear" and taking up prodigious swaths of his waking hours. His real-life interactions took a dive. "I found that I just spent much more time thinking about the flame wars that I was in than the people that I hung out with," says Barger.

As intense as his netnews involvement was, though, Barger felt something was missing—a context for his postings, some frame of reference that would fill in the contours of his Net persona, now badly fragmented across the boundaries of his various newsgroups. His weblog, in the end, was born to fill that need. It was conceived less as the quality news digest it has become (frequented by thousands of the Net's most knowledgeable) than as a portrait of Jorn Barger, rendered in the medium of his own daily, unexpurgated curiosities. "I was inspired by Ana Voog's Anacam, by the whole aesthetic of being on the Net twenty-four hours a day, and being as transparent as possible," he says. "I try to make it my ethic that whenever I see something that I enjoy, I don't filter. You know, if it's some silly thing about a TV commercial, I won't say, well, that's too frivolous."

Does it even count as irony that Barger's rigorously unfiltered perspective is perhaps as good a filter as can be found for the welter of the Web? It practically goes without saying: Accept that the Web ultimately overwhelms all attempts to order it, as for now it seems we must, and you accept that the delicate thread of a personal point of view is often as not your most reliable guide through the chaos. The brittle logic of the hierarchical index has its indispensable uses, of course, as has the crude brute strength of the search engine. But when their limits are reached (and they always are), only the discriminating force of sensibility will do—and the more richly expressed the sensibility, the better.

In the end, then, there is at least a little something to the claim that weblogs belong to literature. Deriving full-bodied, believable personalities from the quotidian flow of consciousness is, after all, one of literature's specialties—especially the high-modernist literature to which Barger has, not coincidentally, dedicated himself. Whether James Joyce would recognize the traces of his stream-of-consciousness techniques in Robot Wisdom's daily trickle of links is, of course, an open question. But Marcel Proust, who also spent his waking hours in bed compiling an impressive log of life's detail, would certainly approve. And as for that arch-late-modernist Jorge Luis Borges, whose oeuvre is more or less one long meditation on the themes that haunt information fetishists like Barger, don't get me started.

Well, too late. Borges, as it happens, is curiously absent from Barger's constellation of literary heroes, but the truth is, Robot Wisdom's labyrinthine castle of links and annotations would have fit in comfortably among the fables of the *Ficciones*. Barger's passions, like those of Borges, are a librarian's, concerned with superabundances of word and image and the struggle to wrest sense and order from them. Like the hero of Borges's "Funes the Memorious," who suffers from the inability to forget a single thing he's seen or heard, Barger contends daily with a surfeit of memory—the Web's vast, collective store of recollections. Funes ultimately resorts to cataloguing it all in terms of purely personal associations (he even counts in them, replacing numbers with mental hyperlinks: "Luis Melian Lafinur, Olimar, sulphur, the reins, the whale, the gas, the cauldron, Napoleon, Augustin de Vedia," and on toward infinity). And so, too, in effect, does Barger.

The difference being this, of course: where Funes is a tragic figure, unable in the end to make anything of the chaos but more chaos, Barger has made of it a cabinet of wonders. As all good bloggers do.

The State of the Blog
Part 1: Blogger Past
....

Giles Turnbull
February 26, 2001

EVAN WILLIAMS,[1] HIS COMPANY PYRA,[2] AND ITS PRODUCT BLOGGER,[3] have come a long way in the last two years. He kindly agreed to answer questions in an email interview with *WriteTheWeb*, in which we asked for his views on the state of the weblogging scene. This is the first of three parts which will appear during the course of this week.

Pyra itself has had a rough ride in recent months. It made a (hugely successful) appeal for funds from Blogger users, but eventually had to lose all staff except Williams himself, who now runs a much simpler and quieter operation single-handed.

Our questions were divided into three sections: Blogger past, Blogger present, and Blogger to come. This first section deals with Blogger's past.

WriteTheWeb: OK, simple to start with—what date did Blogger go live?
Evan Williams: Looking back on Evhead,[4] it looks like it was August 23, 1999.
WtW: Can you remember how you felt at the time? How much work had gone into building it at that point? Did you

just feel relieved to get it out in the open, or nervous, or what?

EW: We were excited at the time, but not overwhelmingly nervous or anything. As you may have read elsewhere, we considered Blogger just a small side project at the time. What we were really working on was a much more complex groupware/website management product (called Pyra).

We put up Blogger just because we thought it'd be a simple little thing that was useful to a few people and, eventually, maybe we could upgrade them to Pyra. Since Blogger was based largely on code we had already written (both for our own blogs and for Pyra), the first version only took about a week of just Paul's and my time, to go from design to launch.

When it got linked to by some of the most well-read blogs at the time—memorably, Peterme[5] and Scripting News[6]—we were quite excited.

WtW: What was the inspiration behind building Blogger? Can you remember how it all came together in your minds?

EW: I actually had the idea for Blogger several months before we decided to build it. All of us in the company (just Meg, Paul, and myself at the time) were publishing our own sites as weblogs. Being Web developers, we naturally wrote our own code to automate the publishing of these sites.

Having done this, we realized how powerful it was to publish something on your site with such ease and immediacy. We knew that some people did blogs by hand, but I couldn't imagine why you would bother.

The seed of the idea for launching Blogger as a Web app, though, came when Paul wrote a script to publish our external company blog by writing out a static file and FTPing it to our Pyra.com server (which we didn't have database access on at the time).

At first, we put off building the tool because it just seemed like one of many good ideas, and we felt we needed to focus (which was true). Then, we found some way to justify it and did it anyway.

WtW: More importantly, perhaps, did you have any inkling of what the reaction would be?

EW: While it seemed like a useful little tool, we certainly did not account for the enthusiasm it would generate. We kept trying to go back and work on our "real" product, because Blogger just didn't seem that significant. But Blogger would not be denied our attention.

WtW: Have blogs developed in the way you expected? Did you allow yourselves any expectations?

EW: I would like to claim it was inspired genius from the beginning, but not at all. Personally, it took me a long time to realize what was so significant about both the blog format and the tool itself.

It was only after I put the Pyra product, which contained (to me) important ideas I'd been thinking about for years, on hold that I started to realize the full scope of what was happening with blogs and Blogger.

WtW: Can you give us some indication of the growth of user numbers over time?

EW: For the first couple months, we got 10–20 new users a day. We launched a new version in November of '99, after which we got a relatively large influx and were up to about 2,300 by the end of the year. Through last year, we averaged 20 to 40 percent growth per month, and that continues today. As of right now, there are 117,970 registered users. 19,582 of those signed up in January.

The State of The Blog
Part 2: Blogger Present

Giles Turnbull

February 28, 2001

WtW: When you meet a complete stranger on the bus, someone who knows what the Web is but has never seen a blog, how do you describe what you do, and what Blogger is?

EW: I stammer a lot. I guess I've never really had a great answer to that question. I usually say Blogger is a Web publishing tool, mostly for personal and independent publishers, that takes the tediousness and technicality out of adding things to websites.

If they are still interested, I usually try to find an example they'd be familiar with—most of the time, people get the idea of a "What's New" page. I often use that to explain what blogs are.

WtW: In your minds, is Blogger about content management, personal publishing, data management, all three, or something else?

EW: At various times—mostly because I was thinking about payroll and impressing investors—I've shied away from the "personal publishing" label, but these days I fully embrace it. To me, that's what is important and exciting about Blogger—it empowers personal publishers.

Within that realm, it's about content management—specifically, *lightweight* content management—the big, embarrassingly gaping hole still yet to be filled in order to make the vision of the Web democratizing media a reality.

WtW: Do you think the blog concept has become stale? Was there ever a "blog concept" in the first place?

EW: To me, the blog concept is about three things: Frequency, Brevity, and Personality. These are the three characteristics that I believe are the driving factors in weblogs' popularity as a publishing format. This clarification has evolved over time, but I realized early on that what was significant about blogs was the format—not the content.

I always chided against the early definition of weblogs as link lists or annotations of the Web. This was largely how weblogs were defined—even by us, at first—and partially led to the trivialization of the format by a lot of Internet "old-timers." I think it's pretty widely accepted at this point that the definition is broader—that the "blog concept" is mostly about frequently posting chunks of content on a webpage and organizing it chronologically.

So, to answer the second question, I do think there was *a* blog concept. Then there were a couple blog concepts. And now we're getting closer to *a* blog concept again.

Is this concept getting stale? Like anything, over time it's lost its newness and on-the-cutting-edge feel. It's much easier to feel like you're tuned in to something exciting when just a few insiders are doing it than when it's done by 50,000 tech-savvy teens and their not-so-tech-savvy grandmas.

But I'm convinced that we are still at the very beginning. The concept will continue to become more prevalent, to the point where it probably won't even be talked about—simply because it is the native format for publishing all kinds of information on the Web.

Blogs will become the default format for personal sites (which, despite the dot-com collapse and the inability for anyone to make money off them, continue to grow at a phenomenal rate—both in terms of numbers and centrality to people's lives), and they will become a staple of professional publishers' and business sites, as well.

WtW: Would you like to see different uses of Blogger, or do you think that depends on upgrades to the feature set?

EW: I'm not terribly concerned with seeing different uses of Blogger. Regarding the feature set, that is one thing which, I have to admit, has gotten a little stale.

Blogger hasn't evolved nearly as quickly as I would have hoped or expected. There is a tremendous amount to be done—which will shepherd in many exciting new uses—but we were just too stretched, too unfocused, and too overwhelmed with scaling and other issues to ever get the really interesting stuff we've been dying to do forever out the door. (That is changing now.)

WtW: There's a lot of talk and anticipation about Blogger Pro. What can you tell us will be in it—and crucially, what will it cost?

EW: Yeah, well, hmmm . . . Blogger Pro has been on and off the front burner so many times, it's embarrassing. We've had a set of features, which we defined as Blogger Pro, in beta for two or three months.

We've never launched them publicly and for pay for various reasons—largely, when I had the rest of the team, it was because the resources we felt it would take to finish, launch, maintain, and support it were not going to pay for themselves anytime soon, and we, therefore, needed to focus on bigger deals.

At this point, my plan is still to eventually offer various subscription-based services, such as Pro. But obviously my resources for providing a professional-level service have somewhat decreased, and I have a bit of work to do before I feel comfortable offering something I'm making people pay for.

In general, I'm reassessing everything—business strategy and technology-wise—so I can't say right now when Pro will rear its head, in what form, or for how much money.

WtW: What has Blogger done for Pyra?

EW: Blogger has become Pyra.

WtW: Your request for donations proved extremely successful. How did that affect the way you think about your users?

EW: I was overwhelmed by the response to the Server Fund. Not only did it generate much more money than we anticipated (a total of about $12,000 from users at this point—plus another $4,500 from *Web Techniques* magazine), the kind words and offers to help were both humbling and inspiring.

It demonstrated my belief that people were willing to pay for things that mattered to them on the Web—and invigorated my commitment to keeping Blogger alive. It was also interesting how the contributions were dispersed. In actuality, a very tiny percentage of Blogger users gave anything at all.

But the average donation was much greater than I would have ever guessed. Some people were amazingly generous. Of course, this is both bad and good. It may show that a few people are extremely willing to pay—but not enough to make things viable.

WtW: Is Blogger now financially secure, or might you have to ask for help again? Presumably you have significant server-side costs that can only increase as the number of users increases.

EW: The hosting costs are a tiny fraction of what the payroll was, which made up 90 percent of our overhead until recently, so I don't have near the financial pressure I felt before.

On the other hand, it's still rather significant for a service that is not currently producing any income and a company that is out of funding. Plus, you're right, these costs are only increasing. The good news is, I have some deals in the works that should put me in good standing for at least the rest of the year.

By that time, I expect Blogger to be sustainable unto itself.

WtW: Are you able to name any sites where you have noticed particularly unusual/interesting/different use of Blogger?

EW: We tried to highlight such sites with our Blog of the Week,[1] which features sites like Who Would Buy That,[2] which, with much humor, highlights odd items for sale on eBay; the Press Nothing to Continue[3] episode of 0sil8, which hooked up Blogger to Tellme,[4] so you can listen to a blog over the phone; and Presidential Haiku,[5] which features, well, haikus about American presidents.

The State of the Blog
Part 3: Blogger Future
....

Giles Turnbull

March 2, 2001

WtW: What else do you see yourselves doing with the technology, apart from growing capacity?

EW: Beyond simple UI enhancements and power features, I'm interested in two general areas:

1) Utilizing the Network. That is, taking Blogger beyond a simple tool that offers an alternative to putting your own database and script behind your site, to taking advantage of the fact that I have thousands of sites being published through a central system on a constant basis.

I.e., doing things along the lines of distributed community and content aggregation to help readers find more content they're interested in, writers find more of the natural audience for their content, and people to connect with like-minded people.

2) Making Blogger Extensible. I absolutely love the idea of programmable, extensible Web services. I desperately want to open Blogger up and let other people plug their tools and interfaces into it.

We've actually had an XML-RPC-like interface to Blogger for several months. We never opened it up for lack of both a clear business model on how to do so and because, when you're having scaling problems, it doesn't really make a lot of sense to open up your servers to potentially do a lot more things—and with less control.

This is something I will definitely get back to, though.

WtW: Have you thought of taking the cybermapping approach and allowing blogs to be selected by location on a map?

EW: I haven't thought a lot about it, but I'd love to see it. Better directory features in general are something we (and the blogging community as a whole) desperately need.

WtW: What new features are most requested by users?

EW: Spellchecking, archive templates, picture support, email out . . .

WtW: And linked to that, what features are *you* most interested in adding?

EW: Hmmm . . . so many. At the top of the list would probably be things like comments (i.e., readers can make comments on posts—*à la* BlogVoices) and email in and out.

Thinking bigger, I'm dying to allow bloggers to syndicate each other's stuff (i.e., see utilizing the network).

WtW: How do you think blogging will change in the next five years?

EW: I guess we'll probably be blogging from hovercrafts and wearing shiny suits.

WtW: Do you have any plans to move the app to the desktop?

EW: I don't plan to *move* the app to the desktop, but I do plan to *extend* it to the desktop. In the midst of the p2p hype these days, I think a lot of the beautiful advantages of web applications are getting forgotten about.

Applications delivered over the Web still have big advantages in terms of accessibility-from-anywhere, maintainability, ease-of-adoption, collaboration, and multiplatform support. However, there are obvious advantages to a decentralized approach, as well.

I'm shooting for a best-of-both-worlds architecture, which will include optional desktop (and "satellite" server) tools.

WtW: With that in mind, do you worry that Blogger might face competition from improved desktop-based authoring software?

EW: I'm sure it will. But as I implement some of the ideas around utilizing the network, as I mentioned above, I think it will be clear that the software+service approach is a powerful combination that completely "detached" software can't match.

My hope, of course, is that we can collaborate. In fact, just the other day, I met with one of the leading web tools vendors about how they can hook their desktop apps to Blogger. That, I think, would be the best of both worlds.

14

The Kaycee Nicole (Swenson) FAQ

Adam Geitgey

May 22, 2001

WELCOME TO THE KAYCEE NICOLE (SWENSON) FAQ VERSION 0.7

This document attempts to explain what is currently known about the Kaycee Nicole Cancer Hoax and how the MetaFilter.com community uncovered these facts.

If you are researching this story, please read this document to get an idea of what is going on. Remember: the Web isn't evil, evil people are evil.

All the references you can handle and then some are at: http://groups.yahoo.com/group/kaycee-nicole/links

Part 1: Summary—What Exactly Happened?

For more than two years, a sizable group of Internet users were caught up in the story of Kaycee Nicole. She was an attractive High School/College student dying from leukemia and she kept users updated via her online diary. Eventually her mom also started a companion diary to express the feelings associated with caring for a child with cancer. Many people became close friends with Kaycee Nicole through email, chat room, and even phone conversations. When Kaycee finally succumbed, her online friends grieved like they had lost members of their own families. Well, there is one problem. Kaycee Nicole never existed.

Here is what almost certainly happened according to the original facts, MetaFilter users' investigations, and a reporter who is investigating this matter:

Kelli Swenson was a middle schooler in the Oklahoma City metro area. She, probably with her friends, created an imaginary girl named Kaycee Nicole around 1997 or 1998. They made a series of personal webpages for the new girl to give her a life of her own. Kaycee's first website was on the same Geocities account as Kelli's own page, but other Kaycee homepages were made with basically repetitive information. There was no mention of cancer. Kelli used pictures of a local high school basketball star to give Kaycee the face of an attractive young girl. The person in the pictures (now a college basketball player) is not involved in any way.

At some point, Kelli's real-life mother Debbie Swenson found about about the imaginary person that her daughter and friends had created. She, for whatever reason, took over and turned Kaycee into a leukemia victim. Somewhere around this time, Kaycee joined the CollegeClub website. Kaycee told her stories of suffering from cancer and and became a popular member of the CollegeClub community. Staff members became close friends and traded care packages with the Swenson family. Kaycee Swenson was even quoted in a *New York Times* article about college life.

The story really begins with Randall van der Woning. He became friends with Debbie and thus Kaycee through John Halcyon's citizenx website. He runs a weblog called "adventures of a big white guy living in hong kong" and he offered to personally set up a weblog for Kaycee so that she could share her love and experiences with others. Unfortunately for Randall, his new friend and source of inspiration didn't exist.

Kaycee Nicole's new weblog became popular. The love and fearlessness displayed by a dying girl was inspirational. All of the weblog entries were actually written by Debbie Swenson. Debbie weaved a tale of remission and recurrence that kept well-wishers locked on to the site. As imaginary Kaycee's overall condition deteriorated, her new friends did what would be expected. They sent cards, gifts, and possibly money. What exactly became of these gifts is not certain at this time, but Debbie never explicitly asked for gifts to be sent.

On Randall's suggestion, Debbie started her own weblog. She wrote of the pain experienced raising a daughter who she knew would probably die. Debbie gave detailed accounts of everything that happened to Kaycee, but most disturbingly she assimilated Kaycee into stories about her own real life children. When she discussed her two real kids, she would tell how they felt about Kaycee, how much they looked up to her, how worried they were, and so on. The level of detail is amazing.

After a few years, Debbie apparently decided that this had dragged on long enough. Just when Kaycee looked to be beating cancer, Debbie said she had an aneurysm and that she had died. The community outpouring of support was remarkable and those who knew Kaycee well suffered serious bouts of grief. This is also when larger suspicious arose. Debbie refused to provide an address to send cards or condolences, would not provide any real information about a funeral, and basically provided no real evidence that anyone had died. Most people believed that Kaycee was real because no one would attempt such a massive ongoing hoax. That was the stuff of outlandish conspiracy theories. Supporters assumed that the family just wanted to maintain an appropriate level of privacy. But a MetaFilter post questioning the existence of Kaycee was the key to the undoing of the whole mystery. Participants in the MetaFilter discussion began searching for proof of Kaycee's existence. None could be found. Even worse, evidence of a hoax emerged. After an intense and impressive community investigation, most of the facts became clear. Debbie admitted she wrote everything, though the details of her confession are questionable. Debbie refuses to reveal who provided Kaycee's voice for those who spoke with her on the phone.

Part 2: The Players—Who Did What?

Kaycee Nicole Swenson—A figment of Kelli Swenson's imagination who was turned into a leukemia victim by Kelli's mom, Debbie Swenson. Debbie claims in her confession that Kaycee is a character that represents three real life cancer victims and was used to telling their stories. She also claimed that the photos of Kaycee were really those of a cancer victim who was one of the three people that made up Kaycee's online personality. It has been proven that the photos are of a girl still living and who has nothing to do with any of this. As such, most assume that Kaycee was actually a reflection of Debbie and her daughter with other tidbits thrown in, not the condensed story of anyone directly.

Debbie Swenson—The woman who made up everything that happened to Kaycee. This is the hoaxer. The amount of detail she provided and the way she wove Kaycee into her life is disturbing. She reportedly believes she did nothing wrong in all of this.

Kelli Swenson—Debbie's real life daughter. She created Kaycee originally and was probably involved heavily throughout Kaycee's existence. One person who called Kaycee reports that Kelli answered and handed the phone to Kaycee. This is how the daughter was originally brought into suspicion of being part of the hoaxing herself.

Randall van der Woning—The man who set up and hosted Kaycee and Debbie's weblogs. He was a close friend who talked to both often. He had no idea that Kaycee didn't exist. After it was revealed to him that it was all a hoax, he deleted both Kaycee and Debbie's weblogs and posted an explanation.

John "Halcyon" Styn—an "unrelenting extrovert" and generally nice guy who became close friends with Kaycee during his days at CollegeClub. His caring nature led him to unwittingly promote and support the fictional Kaycee. Randall met Kaycee through John's citizenx website which of course led to the whole weblog. Some people originally suspected that John might have been involved in the hoax, but this was completely disproven.

Julie (last name omitted)—A high-school basketball star in Oklahoma. Many photographs of her from year books, basketball games, and the like were used as pictures of Kaycee Nicole. When it was discovered that the Kaycee Nicole pictures were really Julie, there was little doubt left that everything Debbie had said was a lie.

Audra Lea—A girl with a website who didn't even know Kaycee well. Her boyfriend at the time introduced her to the Kaycee story and as a small gift, Audra bought Kaycee the kayceenicole.com domain name. The record of her purchasing the domain name and her general resemblence to the Kaycee pictures led some to believe she was involved in the hoax, but this was quickly disproven.

There were many other people involved: friends of Kaycee, people who helped uncover the hoax in various ways, etc. But those listed were the main players.

Part 3: The Investigation

So how did the Kaycee Nicole story progress from "hard to doubt" to an "obvious hoax"? The answer is that a lot of people worked hard to uncover the truth.

Initial Doubts

A few people had doubted Kaycee's authenticity while she was still "living," but so many people talked to her on a regular basis that these doubts were mostly ignored. The initial impetus of real doubt was a pair of articles posted soon after Kaycee's "death" on personal weblogs spelling out how Kaycee could have been faked. Most of the details of these original posts were inaccurate in hindsight, but the authors had the main idea. This led to a large discussion on the MetaFilter website which in turn led to many people checking out Kaycee's validity.

At this point, most people still believed Kaycee was real. But all that was really known was that a girl named Kaycee Nicole had possibly died in a small town in Kansas.

- When Kaycee's death was announced, the family wouldn't provide an address to send cards. The P.O. Box used in the past was no longer accepting mail.
- People began to realize that NO ONE had actually met Kaycee in real life, even those who had frequent phone conversations with her over the course of several years' time.
- Kaycee often quoted song lyrics in her posts. 1960s and '70s song lyrics. And her posts seemed to be written by someone older than 19.
- No one could find an obituary. One person called the newspaper in Kaycee's small town and they said that they had not heard of any girl with leukemia.
- And most importantly, no one could show that anyone named Kaycee Nicole had lived in Oklahoma or Kansas. High schools tracked down from basketball photos of Kaycee didn't seem to have any students that were named

Kaycee. Various random people named Kaycee found on the Web were suggested, but none of them panned out.

- Finally, someone noticed that the *New York Times* article that quoted Kaycee (and Kaycee linked to it on her site) listed her as Kaycee Swenson. This was the only time a last name for Kaycee was mentioned. Someone turned up a "Kelli Swenson" with a mother named "Debbie Swenson" on the Web. Kaycee's mother's name was Debbie. Kelli was a little too young to be Kaycee, but the other similarities were striking. Kaycee said she lived in Oklahoma and moved to Kansas in 1999. The Swenson family page said they lived in Oklahoma and had an update on the webpage about them moving to Kansas in 1999. The actual cities matched. The only thing not certain is why Kelli was younger than Kaycee.
- The operator of MetaFilter revealed Kaycee's IP address from an email he had gotten from her before she "died." This IP address was from an internet provider in Peabody, Kansas. The same place Debbie Swenson now lives.

The Hoax Is Revealed

The next morning, presumably due to this mounting evidence, Debbie revealed that it was all a hoax. She claimed that she created Kaycee to tell the stories of three cancer victims she had personally known and that the pictures of Kaycee on the Web were of one of those victims. She said that the person pictured was the main basis of Kaycee and that she in fact had died. Debbie admitted writing everything herself.

Randall was crushed. He deleted the weblogs and insisted that Debbie call and explain herself. She told Randall her story, parts of which have been proven to be false. So now we knew it was a hoax. But what wasn't clear was if a 19-year-old had actually died or not. We also still did not know if Debbie herself was a real person. Luckily, her talk with Randall revealed some important information.

Debbie said that Kaycee's last name wasn't Swenson, but instead she had used Debbie's own last name in the *New York Times* to protect her identity. Well, Kaycee didn't do that because she isn't real but this indirectly told us that Debbie's last name WAS Swenson, and thus she was very likely the same Debbie Swenson found earlier. Before this, the last name couldn't be confirmed.

A huge connection was made. Someone noticed that Kelli Swenson's *N'Sync fan page was on the SAME ACCOUNT on Geocities as the oldest Kaycee Nicole (pre-cancer) page. There was little doubt now that we had the wrong Debbie and Kelli.

The Swenson family page had a picture of their old church in Oklahoma. Someone called the pastor listed on the sign in the picture. The pastor confirmed a lot of information that was suspected. He also mentioned very quickly that Debbie LOVED to write poetry. Kaycee was also a huge poetry writer. A poem on the Swenson family page was found to be very similar to one of Kaycee's poems.

So now we know that Debbie IS a real person in Kansas and that she wrote the weblog. But we didn't know if there was or wasn't a dead teenager. We had to prove that the person shown to be Kaycee in all the photos was either dead or alive. Trying to find someone based on a few pictures and no confirmed name can be pretty hard.

- The obvious step was to examine the pictures for any evidence of their origin. Many of the pictures were amateurly edited in a graphics program to remove things like the name of the school on Kaycee's basketball uniform. Someone used Photoshop to enhance a skewed image of the gym floor to uncover that the school's mascot was a lion, but that was little help at this point. We didn't have a confirmed real name for Kaycee and high schools don't usually post pictures of their students on webpages, so we couldn't see who looked like Kaycee.

- Some thought that Audra Lea was the person in the Kaycee pictures. People who really knew Audra, however, said she looked nothing like those pictures in real life.

- Around this time, a live chat room for discussing developments was set up. Work was very collaborative and productive in this environment. Additional Kaycee webpages were found. These pages had more photos. One of these photos clearly showed the school mascot and that Kaycee was #10 on the basketball team. By putting together the mascot in the photo with the city the Swensons were originally from, the school where the photos originated was tracked down. A women's basketball roster for the school in 1999 listed #10 as Julie. Someone immediately typed the full name into Google, and the first link returned was quite eerie. It was Julie's player profile from the college she attends. And clear as day was a picture of "Kaycee Nicole" staring back from the screen.

- The whole situation quickly blew up. Julie was still playing basketball games and wasn't dead. There was now hard evidence that not only was Kaycee Nicole Swenson a fabrication, but she was also not directly based on any mysterious dying teenager. The owner of MetaFilter.com soon after got an email to call a journalist. He called, and the holes were filled in. The journalist had talked to Debbie directly. She told more about what actually happened, but refused to talk about who provided the voice of Kaycee on the phone. She also claims she did nothing wrong.

The Aftermath

- Julie has been contacted. See below. She didn't even know any of this happened. The Swensons were big fans of Julie and Julie gave her the pictures herself. Those pictures were used to create Kaycee.
- Since Julie is alive and well, obviously Debbie's confession that claimed the photos were of a cancer victim are completely false. She can't even confess honestly.
- I've learned that Kaycee wasn't pictured in the *New York Times* article because she claimed to be frail from cancer and didn't want to appear. The paper respected her wishes and didn't try to come take pictures. This info is from the other person (the one pictured) in the *New York Times* article.

What an exciting and weird week.

15

In the Trenches with a Weblog Pioneer: An Interview with the Force Behind Eatonweb, Brigitte F. Eaton

John S. Rhodes
December 7, 1999

Weblogs, Usability, and Beyond

Is usability important for a weblog? Why? Why not?

I think that usability is important on all websites. That said, I don't think usability affects weblogs very much. Since weblogs tend to be a single page that is read and updated daily, there are only two really important things: is it readable, and are the links clearly indicated. Everything else can conceivably be ignored. If a blogger wants their readers to use the rest of their site, however, they'll need to pay attention to the site structure, and navigation along with all the other usability issues.

How do you define content? In your opinion, what things are worth mentioning to readers of a weblog?

Content, for me, is anything that I find interesting, whether it's an article, a personal page, a comic, whatever. That along with my commentary and journal-like entries (which, of course, I think

are very interesting) is what makes up Eatonweb.[1] Since I started
the weblog essentially as a bookmarking tool, things that are
worth mentioning tend to be things that I'd like to find again, articles, studies, etc. and then the odd amusing or weblog-related
link. I try not to consider whether it's "worth mentioning" or not,
just whether I found it interesting.

*How do you know you are in touch with your readers? Do you (and
should you) care about users?*

I know that I'm *not* in touch with my readers at all. I very
rarely hear from them. Several months ago I had an identity cri-
sis where I found myself analyzing each link, trying to decide if
it was interesting enough for my readers. It broke down pretty
quick, and I realized that I weblog for myself, it's somewhere that
I put stuff I'm interested in. A place that I can pour out my feelings, irritations, and ego-filled opinions. I'm still surprised people keep coming back for more.

*What needs to change to make weblogs, in general, more valuable and
useful to users?*

I don't think anything needs to change. As far as I can tell, users
of weblogs find them very valuable as filters of web information. I
could maybe envision a categorization system (sort of like Memepool[2] already does) but one that allows the user to choose which
categories are of interest to them. They could then deselect all my
personal entries and weblog-related entries and just read the entries
that they found value in. Actually Whump[3] already does this, and it
hasn't seemed to propagate, so maybe it's not that important after all.

Inside Eatonweb

What is Eatonweb? What is its purpose? What is your role?

Eatonweb started as an HTML project of my husband's; when he got sick of the novelty, I put up an online portfolio & resume. It was very much a static place until the beginning of this year. I'd been inspired by an article by Lance Arthur in Alistapart[4] telling designers to think outside the box and push the limits of HTML without worrying about backwards compatibility issues. I had the place to do it, and a concept of what I wanted to do, but no content. I ran across both weblogs and online journals about the same time and realized that I'd found my content.

Of course, since that initial design, it's evolved. I've dropped the journal and I added a weblog portal,[5] and for some reason I've now got visitors. Because of those users, the initial concept of pushing the limits has had to be reigned in, but Eatonweb is very much an expression of myself and a place designed to express myself.

What are your skills? What tools do you use to generate Eatonweb?

I've got a really wide range of skills in web development. I've done everything from graphics to Java programming, But what I really enjoy is information design and UI design. As far as Eatonweb, I just use emacs to edit the HTML and then FTP it to my server. I have yet to find any tool that is more convenient or easier for me to use.

Please describe your weblog portal.

My weblog portal[6] started as an attempt to list all the weblogs that were floating around on the Web. I'd been using Cam's list on his site,[7] but he wasn't updating it fast enough for me, so I figured I'd start my own. This was back when there were only 30 or so blogs, and it was pretty easy to maintain. When it hit about 150, Aaron[8] created his Surfmenu[9] so I stole his idea for putting all the weblogs in a JavaScript array. This enabled me to actually

manipulate the data, and provide sorting by category, etc. I gradually realized that people were afraid to send me an email asking
me to add a blog to the list, so I also implemented an anonymous
submission form. Since then it's gone crazy and it's pushing 400
weblogs. What bothers me about the portal, is the fact that I'm
both forcing my categorization system on people, and standing
as judger of whether something is a weblog or not. That's why I
started the openblogportal: it allows people to add their own
blogs and recategorize in ways that make sense to them.

Final Thoughts and Opinions

What makes a weblog worth visiting? What are your favorites?

I find personality and interesting links are what makes a
weblog a good read. Some of my favorites are bifurcated Rivets,[10]
Genehack,[11] Peterme,[12] Evhead,[13] and Lake Effect.[14] Although I
have about 20 daily regulars, including WebWord,[15] they're all
listed in my daily browse clip which I change constantly.

*What does the future hold for weblogs? What's coming soon? What
should we expect?*

I'm sure many people will start a serious push to make profit
from a weblog. I don't know how they'll do it, but I've definitely
seen enough talk floating around. At the minimum you'll probably see a lot more blogs with banner ads, or sponsorships. As
more tools develop to make it easy to create a weblog, we'll see
more and more people who don't know HTML starting up their
own blogs.

When possible, should weblogs be commercial? Why? Why not?

I don't have anything against weblogs that are commercial; the
format makes sense for a lot of business sites as well as personal

sites, and Pyra[16] is a good example. But in some ways commercialization takes away the heart of weblogging, the personality which makes so many blogs enjoyable to read. Then again, maybe I just haven't seen enough good commercial blogs.

Final comments? Shameless plugs? Pearls of wisdom to share?

I think self-publishing is a huge trend which will certainly be growing over the next few years. The Web has enabled people to express themselves to the world in a whole new way. As more tools develop and are improved upon, people with no technical background or interest will have the opportunity to discover this self-expression and at the same time others can take advantage of the relevancy these people create. That's what makes weblogs so wonderful. They're nothing new, they're not changing the world with their content, they're not going to make anyone huge amounts of money, but they are a form of self-expression and community which others enjoy reading.

Brigitte, thank you very much for your insights and opinions.

Blog, Blog, Blog

16

Been 'Blogging'? Web Discourse Hits Higher Level

Glenn Fleishman
April 1, 2001

LINKS BEGET LINKS: THIS IS A TENET OF THE INTERNET.
Every time Net users discover a resource or site of interest, they link to it. Over time, links aggregate and accumulate, and the most linked-to sites become the most popular.

An interesting side effect of this kind of laser-beam pointing has grown into a mature phenomenon in the past year: weblogging, known as "blogging."

Blogging is the art of turning one's own filter on news and the world into something others might want to read, link to, and write about themselves.

[*Blog, blogging* or *blogger*: Take the phrase "Web log" and apply the linguistic behavior known as false splitting—move a letter from one word to another (as "a napron" turned into "an apron")—and you get the phrase, "We blog." Coining generally attributed to Peter Merholz.][1]

Weblogs comprise short or long comments about links to articles, sites, press releases, and discussions. Typically, they're time-bounded and date-stamped, with older entries scrolling off the bottom into chronological archives.

Tens of thousands of users have weblogs, and many update them daily, or even many times a day, with new snippets or writings. Some blogs are closer to public diaries; others, the idiosyncratic or authoritative musings of experts and cranks.

Most online sources point to 1999 as the beginning of widespread blogging, as free online software tools eased the process of creating daily logs without specialized Web knowledge. Blogger,[2] Pitas,[3] and Userland Software's Manilasites[4] offer a variety of blogging options, all characterized by a simple Web form to add and edit items.

Submitting the form adds or updates the entry to the online site, whether hosted on your own website or via a blog-hosting service, such as Manilasites. Page templates can be customized, or left at their minimal defaults. You don't need to know HTML, the coding language of the Web, or even have an understanding of any underpinnings to use these services.

Items in a weblog might be drawn from traditional news sources, techie discussion sites like Slashdot,[5] and even other blogs—a practice known as blogrolling. A blog's popularity derives in part from the fingers pointing from other bloggers.

[*Blogrolling*: Derived from logrolling, a habit of trading favors or praise among artists, critics, or academics. Noted blogger Doc Searls[6] claims credit for spreading the meme; several other bloggers agree.]

Paul Andrews, who recently opted for early retirement as a *Seattle Times* reporter and columnist, is now a freelance technology journalist and regular blogger.[7]

"There's a referential and kind of feedback mechanism that's important in blogging," he said. Print journalists, such as the *San Jose Mercury News* Technology columnist Dan Gillmor[8] have leapt into the fray, often without compensation, practicing an art in public usually reserved for private contemplation or with editors.

Journalists' participation in this medium has sparked articles, including *Newsweek* columnist Deborah Branscum's recent take on its significance. In the navel-gazing nature of blogging, her column provoked much public, blogged gnashing of teeth.

Dave Winer, a software developer and head of Userland Software, which offers free weblog hosting, is generally credited as the first regular and well-read blogger, starting a blog in 1997.[9] His commentary is popular enough to have spawned an evil twin: a nasty daily deconstruction of his remarks, ironically hosted on his own company's weblog service.

Blogging in Action

I started blogging in November 2000[10] and quickly developed blogorrhea, a condition that can be cured only by more of the disease, and the imposition of a kind of external discipline on a writer that depends on the growth of actual readers of one's blog.

[*Blogorrhea*: a tendency for creativity-strapped bloggers to write meaningless prose in an attempt to keep their blog active.]

One experience I had recently illustrates how a blog works. Doc Searls recently posted musings[11] about whether Google's[12] hiring Eric Schmidt as chairman might result in the purchase of the search engine by Sun Microsystems, a company Schmidt helped found. I sent Searls some pithy comments and a number of others did the same. Searls posted an update the next day with our responses.[13] He also linked to an online-only column by Branscum at *Fortune* magazine's site about Google's success working with online advertisers.

This kind of mild dust-up happens all the time, with a mix of journalists, ordinary readers, and subject experts responding to their colleagues with no intermediation, and little compunction.

These responses are incorporated into blogs, resulting in more cross-links and a richer vein of detail.

When I write for a mass-market publication, I have no idea how many people actually read the article. When I blog, I can see statistics. My words in print are just a few out of tens of thousands, and as ephemeral as newsprint or glossy paper. Andrews explained, "As a newspaper writer, you know you're reaching a broad audience, but you don't get the feedback effect."

In the blog, however, not only is my blog entirely my own, but my words persist in simple archives, which typically are better indexed by search engines than the databases that print publications maintain online. In some cases, older writing becomes more popular than newer writing.

More Than Musings

Perhaps this is one reason why blogging rose so quickly. It's one thing to push words out on random pages. It's another to be able to archive, sort, and respond to brief snippets and longer essays. The structure enables readers to have a more direct relationship with the writer that builds over time.

Gillmor, speaking at Buzz 2001, looks to his blogging to make his writing for print even more informed by a broader array of opinion. Gillmor writes his blog as part of his staff position at the *Mercury News*, and turns out columns based on this work. "Re-purposing from print to online is the wrong direction," he said, adding, "I want people to basically have a conversation with me." He asserted that results in better journalism.

The immediate future brings a higher potential of turning bloggers into the equivalent of syndicated writers with Userland Software's release in March of Radio Userland.[14] The software allows a user to "tune" into blogs using features that Microsoft is using as the basis of its .NET initiative; it also features a simple blog tool for posting entries.

A user can subscribe via Radio to blogs and conventional news sources that provide the feed in the right format. Radio schedules regular updates, with a default of one hour, providing a constantly refreshed custom "newspaper" with your own personal columnists and sources.

Journalists have yet to figure out how to make money from this medium. Gillmor and Jim Romenesko[15] are two of the only writers paid to write blogs. "Eventually, there will be some new kinds of economic models emerging from the Web" that will make it possible to get revenue from this kind of pure writing, Andrews said.

But, for now, we blog because we can, and because we must.

Linking 1–2–3

Lawrence Lee
December 7, 1998

IF YOU'VE BEEN FOLLOWING TODAY'S LINKS FOR THE PAST MONTH you've seen the results of my work to compile and select links on several different topics about the Web. It's an interesting process to track down links using several different methods and to see how it fits in with how sites are built and content published.

Fishing Holes

I don't have a news ticker that pushes me all the content that makes up Today's Links. So it's a mix of luck, experience and finding some new toys . . . a lot like fishing. There are a few regular spots where I usually start off at to get a feel for what stories are developing. Two of those regular spots are News.Com and *ZDNet News*. Both sites provide a unique service to let their readers know about stories that are still being finished off before the complete story is published. In most cases, I won't even link in the first story I see on a subject until I see what coverage other sites are providing. *Industry Standard* has an interesting exercise with Media Grok where they take a few stories and look at what kind of coverage different sites devoted and how they approached the story. On a more limited basis, you can also find larger sites playing the linking game with News.Com, *Wired*,

ZDNet, and other sites all devoting some space for links to stories from other sites. They seem to understand the value as well.

Lists of Lists

Mailing lists. The reason I'm swamped with hundreds of emails a week. But there are some lists where I usually read to find an occasional interesting link or story. You'll be deleting a lot of messages on a high traffic list, but if there are some well-connected people subscribed, then it should be worth the time.

One alternative is A List Apart[1] that is unique with a moderated digest of new threads and responses on everything to do with the Web. Every few days there will be a digest of selected new topics and responses to previous topics. It's not real time, but that can be a good thing. Also in email, I subscribe to newsletters and a few sites to get notified by email when there's new content available. Though I tend to visit sites at routine times to get new stories linked into Today's Links before I even get a notification message from the site.

How Do I Link This?

Some sites just like to make it hard to link to an article with content being posted to generic pages that will surely be replaced in a few days. Most sites generate content and direct it into a page with a unique name with an index somewhere else that lists the stories. But there are several sites where content is featured on generic pages that are constantly replaced with new content. So they'll have a todaystories.html file that is constantly updated with the newest content and it's hit and miss if you can find an archive when the content is replaced.

There are two sites that are at least making some attempts to accommodate linking that will continue to work a week later.

First, AdAge provides content on generic pages but at the time of publication they also make the archives available. And to go the extra mile, they split up the content into individual stories even though it is presented as a single compilation of stories on the generic page. Another beautiful example is Peter Merholz's site peterme.com where he posts pieces on the front page but dutifully includes a link to the permanent residence at the same time. I talked about getting notified when sites update new content by email, but I also subscribe to sites with Internet Explorer 4.0 to tell me when a page is updated. Well, with sites starting to drop static pages, IE4's method for subscribing to a site of checking time stamps on an HTML file seems to be a fading solution.

Microcontent

I usually link in stories with the title as the only hypertext anchor along with the publication name up front. So I can understand what Jakob Nielsen was talking about with his Alertbox article on microcontent. In certain situations, I know that if I just post the title as a hyperlink that readers will have a small mystery on what the story is about. So I'll include some additional details after the hyperlink: author's name, brief description, or comments.

Even knowing that I selected the links might be of some comfort to readers, but it's something that I want to keep an eye on when I link into Today's Links.

JIT-SE

A good acronym, just-in-time search engines (JIT-SE) which was coined by Dave Winer are search engines that search selected sites and create an index on a timely basis. Two JIT-SEs are offshoots of regular search engines with NewsTracker[2] from Excite and NewBot[3] over at HotWired's HotBot.

NewsTracker beats NewBot hands down with the number of sites it compiles for its JIT-SE and the different topics covered. But like regular search engines, JIT-SEs aren't perfect. On News-Tracker, when I do a search for WebTV, I'll always see pages from *CBS Sportsline*. Why? Well, there's some JavaScript on all the *CBS Sportsline* pages that mention WebTV.

It isn't a new problem to JIT-SEs or regular search engines because you can see NewsTracker's problems documented in the DaveNet on JIT-SE from July 1997. The problem is only magnified when you jump from the limited sources that a JIT-SE looks after to the regular search engines ploughing through the Web. Something that I've been playing with recently are compilation sites that flirt with the role of a JIT-SE. Two that I know of are NewsHub[4] and Newslinx.[5] Newslinx, which was purchased in November by Mecklermedia's Internet.Com, seems to be compiled by hand, while you can see NewsHub bring in new headlines every 15 minutes.

Like JIT-SEs, it's an important consideration to see what publications these compilation sites are covering, so you don't miss out on stories not being indexed by these sites.

That's All?

I hope you start to use some of the tools discussed like News-Tracker, because it really does solve some problems as a JIT-SE. I have it hooked into IE4 so in my address bar I just type "nt webtv" and my search gets passed to NewsTracker and I see the 1000 hits from *CBS Sportsline*.

While discussion on how to improve search engines and JIT-SE continues, maybe you can learn about microcontent and consider how you can improve a site you're working on.

Off to find some more links for Today's Links!

The Internet Is Not Killing Off Conversation but Actively Encouraging It

Douglas Rushkoff
June 29, 2000

HOWEVER VEHEMENTLY TODAY'S WEB ENTHUSIASTS PROCLAIM THAT "content is king," I suspect very few have stopped to consider just what this stuff called content really is. If it's anything at all.

Take any well-branded cereal, for instance, one of those packages of sugar-coated corn meal with a recognizable cartoon character mascot on the box. What's the content there: the cereal, or the cartoon character?

Is the animal cartoon a communicator of the product's brand image, or is the food itself merely a medium through which the character is communicated? It's a tricky distinction. When my father was growing up, bubblegum companies competed by offering free trading cards inside their packages. Little pieces of cardboard with the images of baseball players proved the most successful, and soon children were buying whole packs of baseball cards with only a single stick of bubble gum.

Today, baseball cards are sold without any bubblegum at all. Despite gum's textural attributes, baseball cards proved to be the "stickier" content. Why? Because it provides a richer media experience. Not only can collectors look at pictures, but they can compare and analyze the statistics of each player as chronicled on the card's back.

More importantly, this depth of data allows the card to serve as what I've started to call "social currency." While children can debate the merits of one brand of gum over another for only so long, they can talk endlessly about the players' whose cards they've collected, trade them, or even just peruse one another's collections.

See, the cards aren't really ends in themselves; they are the basis for human interaction. Johnny got some new cards, so the other kids come over to see them after school. The cards are social currency.

We think of a medium as the thing that delivers content. But the delivered content is a medium in itself. Content is just a medium for interaction between people. The many forms of content we collect and experience online, I'd argue, are really just forms of ammunition—something to have when the conversation goes quiet at work the next day; an excuse to start a discussion with that attractive person in the next cubicle: "Hey! Did you see that streaming video clip at streamingvideoclips.com?"

Social currency is like a good joke. When a bunch of friends sit around and tell jokes, what are they really doing? Entertaining one another? Sure, for a start. But they are also using content—mostly unoriginal content that they've heard elsewhere—in order to lubricate a social occasion. And what are most of us doing when we listen to a joke? Trying to memorize it so that we can bring it somewhere else. The joke itself is social currency.

"Invite Harry. He tells good jokes. He's the life of the party."

Think of this the next time you curse that onslaught of email jokes cluttering up your inbox. The senders think they've given you a gift, but all they really want is an excuse to interact with you. If the joke is good enough, this means the currency is valuable enough to earn them a response.

That's why the most successful TV shows, websites, and music recordings are generally the ones that offer the most valuable forms of social currency to their fans. Sometimes, like with mainstream media, the value is its universality.

In the U.S. right now, the quiz show "Who Wants To Be A Millionaire?" is enjoying tremendous ratings because it gives its viewers something to talk about with one another the next day. It's a form of mass spectacle. And, not coincidentally, what is the object of the game? To demonstrate one's facility with a variety of forms of social currency!

Contestants who can answer a long stream of questions about everything from sports and movies to science and history are rewarded with a million dollars. They are social currency champions. Content on the Web is no different. Sure, the Internet allows people to post their own content or make their own websites.

But what do most people really do with this opportunity? They share the social currency they have collected through their lives, in the form of Britney Spears fan sites or collections of illegally gathered MP3s of popular songs. The myth of the Internet—and one I believed for a long time—is that most people really want to share the stories of their own lives.

The fact that "content is king" proves that they don't. They need images, stories, ideas, and sounds through which they can relate to one another. The only difference between the Internet and its media predecessors is that the user can collect and share social currency in the same environment. Those of you who think you are creating online content take note: your success will be directly dependent on your ability to create excuses for people to talk to one another. For the real measure of content's quality is its ability to serve as a medium.

19

Credo of the Web Log Writer

GeekMan at themightygeek.com
October 31, 2001

I WANT TO BE A WEB LOG WRITER.

I will create an ugly website using warez software and ad-infested free web hosts.

I will write something every other day about my boring and uninteresting life.

I will write in "Hackerese" and forego the use of initial caps, for caps are for the weak and non-l337.

I will become an avid reader, loyal fan, and devout worshipper of the most popular "A-List" Web Log Writers.

I will learn how to do what they do, only not as well.

I will purchase gifts for them via PayPal and their Amazon Wish Lists.

I will frequent their CafePress stores.

I will submit my site for review by any Internet critic with a website.

I will not become discouraged when they fail to reply to my emails or notice my website or me.

I will never give up in my quest.

I will become a Web Log Writer.

I will buy my own domain and create a new website of depth and beauty.

I will write something every day about my boring yet somehow compellingly interesting life.

I will reacquaint myself with the 'shift' button and stop spelling words in "Hackerese," for that is for the young and immature.

I will create links to "A-Listers" in the hopes of being noticed.

I will do what they do, only better.

I will create my own PayPal account and Amazon Wish List.

I will open a CafePress store.

I will forego sleep and my weekends because I value my small, yet growing, readership.

I will get average reviews from minor website critics.

I will work hard and garner a loyal following whose ranks will grow larger every day.

I will become an "A-List" Web Log Writer.

I will be featured in a book or magazine.

I will write something every few days about my exciting and interesting life, and my words will be as gospel to the unwashed masses.

I will write poetry and buy a webcam.

I will only link to other "A-List" Web Log Writers and ignore wannabes who link to me.

Other Web Log Writers will do what I do, only worse.

I will ignore or quit my real job since my loyal readership will support me via PayPal and my Amazon Wish List.

CafePress will make me a "Featured Store."

I will be on every critic's favorites list.

I will ignore my readership and become involved in an Internet romance or attend live meetings with other "A-List" Web Log Writers.

I will stop caring about my visitors because they're not worth my time.

I will be a "Has-Been" Web Log Writer.

I will become disillusioned by Web Log Writing and the Internet in general.

I will write a poignant, sarcastic, mean-spirited farewell entry to alienate any visitors I might have left.

I will let my site rot and my links die.

Other Web Log Writers will do what I used to do, only better.

I will find a new job because my Internet romance will die and the other "A-List" Web Log Writers will stop calling me.

I will be forced to close my CafePress store due to inactivity.

I will not be on anyone's favorites list, not even my own.

I will come to the realization that I miss the life of a Web Log Writer.

I will create a new pseudonym and persona to shield myself from recognition.

I will begin my quest anew.

For I want to be a Web Log Writer.

20

The Blogger Code

Ron Yeany
January 9, 2002

GEEKS[1] HAVE ONE. SO DO HAIRY GAY MEN[2] AND THEIR ADMIRERS. Isn't it time bloggers have a code to describe themselves as well? (OK, so maybe not, but we charge forward nonetheless). Answer the following baker's dozen questions. Select the answer in each category that best describes you. The code will only be as accurate as you are truthful. (Skip the question to leave any quotient out of your code.)

B The Blogging [quotient /]

Does longevity equal respect in the blogging world? How long have you been regularly maintaining a personal weblog or online journal?

- ❏ 1–3 months [B1]
- ❏ 3–6 months [B2]
- ❏ 6–9 months [B3]
- ❏ 9–12 months [B4]
- ❏ 1–1½ years [B5]
- ❏ 1½–2 years [B6]
- ❏ 2–2½ years [B7]

❑ 2½–3 years [B8]
❑ over 3 years [B9]

D The Domain [quotient /]

If you don't have your own domain name, does that make you uncool? How many domains do you own?

❑ I own 2 or more domains that are updated regularly. [d++]
❑ I own 2 or more domains, but only one is updated regularly. I just bought the other domain(s) because I made up a cool name. [d+]
❑ I own 1 domain and keep my blog and any other content I produce on the same site. [d]
❑ I don't own a domain, but I have my own web address at blogspot, diaryland, livejournal, or other similar site. [d-]
❑ What's a domain? [d--]

T The Technical [quotient /]

Do you know the difference between XHTML and the XFL? Does "php" sound dirty or illicit to you? Have you ever used the words "closing tag" in a joke?

❑ I maintain and manage my blog with my own home-grown content management system. [t++]
❑ I manage my blog with Greymatter,[3] Movable Type,[4] or other management system running on my own web host. [t+]

❏ I use Blogger,[5] BigBlogTool,[6] upsaid[7] or other similar service to update a site on my own web host. [t]

❏ I use Blogger, BigBlogTool, or similar service to update a
blogspot,[8] Geocities, or other hosted site; or I use diaryland,[9] livejournal,[10] or another service with built-in updating and content management. [t-]

❏ I'll consider myself lucky if I don't get an error while filling
out this form. [t--]

𝕂 The Linkslut [quotient /]

Is the blogging community just one big mutual admiration society? If I scratch your back, will you scratch mine?

❏ I have so many links I couldn't possibly read them all on a
regular basis and/or I nearly always add a link to a site that
has linked to mine. [k++]

❏ I have quite a few links, and I try to check in on them all
regularly, or at least periodically. [k+]

❏ I link only to sites I like to read (and sites that I have time
to read) on a regular basis. [k]

❏ I don't have many links on my site and/or my links are primarily non-blog related [k-]

❏ I don't have any links. Why would I want people to leave
my site? [k--]

𝕊 The Stats [quotient /]

Do you start to worry if your visitors don't keep coming back for
more? How important are the numbers to you?

❏ I check my stats at least once a day, keep my results in a spreadsheet, and/or can tell you my average daily and monthly visitors without having to look it up. [s++]

❏ I usually check my stats once a day but I don't keep any records or running tallies. [s+]

❏ I check my stats occasionally, mostly to discover new blogs that are linking to mine. [s]

❏ I've looked at my stats reports, but I can't remember the last time I checked them. [s-]

❏ What? You mean someone keeps track of how many people visit my site? [s--]

Ⓤ The Usual Suspect [quotient /]

The "Sirs" and "Dames" of the blogging world: bradlands.com, camworld.com, evhead.com, haughey.com, kottke.org, megnut.com, plasticbag.org, powazek.com, rebeccablood.net, saturn.org, scripting.com and zeldman.com,[11] among others. How many of these sites do you link to?

❏ I link to all of them, as well as a few other blog visionaries you left off the list, you idiot. [u++]

❏ I link to many of them mostly because if they ever visit my site I want to make sure they see I have a link to them. [u+]

❏ I link to some of them because I enjoy reading their sites regularly. [u]

❏ Yeah, as if I need to link to their sites . . . if I ever want to visit their site, I'll just follow a link from someone else's blog. [u-]

❏ Never heard of 'em. [u--]

❏ I AM Brad, Cameron, Ev, Matt, Jason, Meg, Tom, Derek, Rebecca, Jack, Dave, or Jeffrey. [u=]

F The Frequency [quotient /]

Do you run your blog, or does your blog run your life? Do you feel as though you are cheating your readers (or cheating yourself) if a day goes by without an update?

- ❏ I update several times a day, every day, and if I don't update, my readers can I assume I'm dead. [f++]
- ❏ I update at least once a day. I can't remember the last day I haven't blogged. [f+]
- ❏ I try to blog once a day, but it doesn't always happen, and that's no big deal. [f]
- ❏ I'm lucky if I manage to post 2 or 3 new entries a week. [f-]
- ❏ Until I started taking this survey, I forgot I had a blog. [f--]

I The Immediacy [quotient /]

Are you usually one of the first to link to the new thing that everyone will be writing about? Are you capable of blogging from just about anywhere at anytime?

- ❏ When I plan something I know will be blog-worthy, I have my laptop or PDA with me so I can blog wirelessly as it's happening. [i++]
- ❏ I sometimes carry a laptop or PDA with me, or I'll find an Internet cafe, and I blog soon after I get an idea. [i+]
- ❏ I blog from either home or work, but only after my work is done and when I get some free time. [i]
- ❏ The blog isn't the first thing I think of, but I usually remember to blog the interesting things . . . eventually. [i-]

❏ I've forgotten to blog something in the past because I forgot about it or never got around to it. [i--]

ⓞ The Originality [quotient /]

Does your blog or journal concentrate on your personal experiences? Do you scour the Web for new and interesting links? Are you happy just adding your comments to the dialogue?

❏ Nearly all the topics I blog are personal experiences or original writing that can't be found elsewhere on the Web. [o++]
❏ I blog some original material with the occasional web link with accompanying personal commentary about the link. [o+]
❏ My entries are a mix of some original material, some web links, and links and comments about other blogs. [o]
❏ I blog mostly links to other web articles and other blogs. [o-]
❏ Are you telling me there are sites other than blogs on the web? [o--]

Ⓧ The Sex [quotient /]

Ah, yes . . . what would a survey be without a sex question? As shocking as it may seem, some bloggers have been known to exchange bodily fluids with one another. What category do you belong to?

❏ I've slept with 2 or more other bloggers (not including significant others), and there are quite a few more I would shag if given the chance. [x++]
❏ I've dated and/or slept with another blogger and/or met my significant other through blogging. [x+]

❑ I haven't bedded another blogger yet, but I certainly wouldn't rule it out if the opportunity presented itself. [x]

❑ I might flirt a little, but anything beyond that is out of the question. [x-]

❑ Are you kidding? The last thing I need is to get sexually involved with one of these neurotic pinheads. [x--]

E The Exhibitionism [quotient /]

With the proliferation of digital cameras, you no longer need be concerned about the clerk at the photo lab seeing your naughty bits. But hell, you'll put on them on your blog. Right?

❑ I have posted several photos of myself on my blog. Some of them may have included full or partial nudity. [e++]

❑ I have posted quite a few photos of myself, but I was fully clothed in them all, thankyouverymuch. [e+]

❑ I have posted at least a photo of my face. [e]

❑ I haven't posted, and don't plan on posting, any photos of myself. [e-]

❑ I've posted a photo of someone else who is more attractive than me and passed it off as my own photo. [e--]

L The Lemming [quotient /]

Do you feel left out if you don't participate in the latest meme or web survey to make the rounds? How compelled are you to follow the pack and do what everyone else is doing?

❑ I rarely find a meme or web survey I don't enjoy, and I find myself blogging the results to most of them. [l++]

❑ I usually check out most of the surveys I run across, but I only blog the results if I find them interesting or favorable. [l+]

❑ I've taken a few surveys or participated in a few memes, but there seem to be so many of them I have to pick and choose. [l]

❑ Memes and web surveys are, for the most part, pretty stupid. Like this survey. [l-]

❑ Did I tell you about the little girl on the bike? [l--]

ℂ The Closet [quotient /]

Can anyone type your name into Google and find your blog? Would you just die (or be fired) if your boss read your blog? Does you mom leave comments on your site?

❑ Nobody I know offline knows about my blog, and I plan on keeping it that way; and/or I blog anonymously. [c++]

❑ Only a few people I know outside of blog circles know about my blog. [c+]

❑ Friends know about my blog, but I generally don't talk about it with some groups (ie: family and/or co-workers) because they probably wouldn't get the whole blogging concept. [c]

❑ There are a few select people I've specifically kept in the dark about my blogging but, for the most part, most people know about it or could easily find it via a web search. [c-]

❑ Nearly all of my offline friends, family members, and co-workers know about my blog, and that's fine. [c--]

Take the letter/character combination at the end of your choices above and string them together to generate your blogger code. Post it on your About Page to show what kind of blogger you are. You can also use one of the many blogger decoders available online.

Weblogs (Good God Y'all) What Are They Good For (Absolutely Nothing—Say It Again)

Neale Talbot
January 15, 2001

FIRSTLY, LET'S GET ONE THING STRAIGHT. WEBLOGGING (OR "BLOGGING") is not a revolution. There is nothing revolutionary about something that's been going on since the Web began.

After all weblogging is, per se, logging things on the Web; and there have always been sites that have achieved this function; can you say "Cool Site of the Day"?

The only difference of late has been the addition of personal commentary and history into the posts, an obvious influence from the equally old Web journals. There is nothing revolutionary about weblogs.

So weblogs, what are they good for?

Since entering the game over a year ago I've heard numerous weblog put-downs: that they add nothing to the Web; that they contribute to the poor writing quality the Internet suffers; that webloggers are all so swept up with inter-linky-loving and referrer stats that they think about nothing else.

These complaints are most likely true; the only people that ever try to refute them are those in the firing line, which might suggest bias on their part.

Then again the bitching often tends to come from webloggers themselves looking for inter-linky-loving goodness and trying to achieve it the easiest way how.

Of course, I've said myself that weblogs are the next Geocities— a badly built, ill-conceived, incestuous bunch of immature websites whose owners have enough self-love to power a small Latin-American coup.

At the same time I love weblogs and run more than a couple myself. But I understand the power of weblogs, the attraction of weblogs and, most importantly, the futility and lack of necessity of weblogs.

For weblogs are, essentially, the most unimportant part of a website. Of the most popular weblogs there are only a couple that are the sole creative outlet for their author. The popular weblogs are, by and large, sidelines to larger works. For instance, Jason Kottke[1] has Osil8,[2] Jeffrey Zeldman[3] has A List Apart,[4] and Heather Champ[5] has Jezebel.[6]

The ironic part is that the most popular weblogs function to serve up the piddle and crap the authors either don't have time for, don't believe worth taking any further, or perhaps are testing the waters for. The most popular weblogs started as junkyards of weblog intelligensia.

What is amusing is the litterboxes are being held up by others as masterpieces despite the rancid smell. Indeed, a whole industry is forming around the fetid heaps of trash that others have left behind. There are now publishers,[7] monitors,[8] and even goddamn awards[9] for the newest form of web waste.

What was once trash in now considered treasure, perhaps even a sport; being the fastest to link,[10] to find the best links,[11] to update the most often,[12] every move you make on your weblog is being measured.

Of course, this sense of competition leads to a sense of importance (or self-importance), a factor only inflated in a terrible
manner by the media, who have fallen into the trap of believing
the future may just be bloggerized.

The media, in its wonder of the instantaneous way petty
thoughts can now reach the Web, has forgotten that personal
publishing on the Web has always been possible; it's now just a
lot easier than before.

With their attention a vicious cycle of hype has started.
Weblogs, once the landfill of the brains of those with better
things to do, have become the voice of a new generation. And
with that, everything the detractors have been bitching about is
coming true; the writing, design and overall quality of weblogs
has dropped since a year ago.

The beautiful thing about this is that it's a natural reaction to
the influx of people with no design or writing skills owning this
"new" technology. And the wonderful thing about that is now
that ordinary people are mimicking the crap of the talented, the
uselessness of weblogs is becoming even more apparent.

What does this mean in the long run? Those that started the
trend will continue to use weblogs as cesspools of the web. Those
that came later will continue their rubbish until it becomes too
much of a pain in the ass and give up. Finally, if the business
community believes the media hype, weblogs will become sani-
tised, corporatised, and so passe that the next generation of
twelve-year-old Internet symbiots will turn up their nose at the
thought of starting one. Then maybe we can get some peace.

PART FOUR
Advice

22

The Four Noble Truths of Blogging

Fishrush

1. PAINFUL MEDIOCRITY (KUTAIFISHI): FISHAKYAMUNI (FISHRUSH) perceived that painfully mediocre blogging is an inevitable part of existence for the normal weblogger and reader of weblogs. He divided the various ways in which we are mediocre into "the Eight Mediocrities" and "the Three Mediocrities."

2. Cause of Painfully Mediocre Blogging (Jittaifishi): When we accumulate delusions and illusions, we create painful mediocrity, which is further created by the three blogging habits:

- Blogging about mental and physical desires, which can be endless
- Blogging about physical objects, one's own ideas, and survival itself
- Blogging about the denial of the value of this temporary existence, which may lead to escapism or nihilism

3. Cessation of Mediocre Blogging (Zeitgeistidiota): Early Fishakyamuni (fishrush) teachings assert that the goal of the blog (and life) is to eradicate the self from the blog, which would lead to a state of perpetuity of the true blogging spirit. Thus, one

would no longer be required to blog about being born into this temporary mediocre blogging state of existence.

4. The Path (drôle la voie d'accès): The practice that Fishakya-muni (fishrush) taught his disciples for the attainment of Blog Enlightenment—called "Matrullo's Decalogue of Blogging Commandments"[1]—is intended to stop them from creating more bad karma and mediocre blogs.

23

Blogma 2001
Missive One: Uphold the Weblog

BLOGMA 2001 Committee
November 14, 2000

(by the way, if you took this seriously, you're an idiot . . .)

BLOGMA 2001'S INITIAL AIM IS TO CIRCUMVENT A CERTAIN EVIL trend that has crept into our once-great weblogging culture: the "celebrity" blogger.

With the advent of tools that make writing and maintaining a weblog possible for anyone with rudimentary computer skills, the democratization of the weblog is in full swing. This is a great and miraculous thing. However, with the increase in size of the weblogging constituency, it is inevitable that it will arouse the attention of the same corporate parasites that have successfully turned other artforms such as music, film, literature, radio, and television into wastelands of the human spirit.

This campaign is targeted at the new bourgeoisie, who even now tag themselves the "A-list" and revel in the circlejerking vacuousness that marks their bilious output. This is an affront to every true weblogger who ever did the hard yards finding gems on the Net that no one else would think of searching for, and bringing them into the light. These decadents, however, have nothing better to do than talk about themselves, and whatever new status symbol they've acquired. Let's point out a prime example, shall we?

Kottke on the tenth of November:[1] "I have completed my quest for a laptop bag. I decided on the Kensington SaddleBag. It has a padded compartment for my laptop, all sorts of neat pockets for Palms, phones, etc . . . "

Need I say more?

And of course every year they rush off to the SXSW conference in Austin, TX (of course the seat of the Texas Death Machine, George W. Bush) and give themselves a good ol' pat on the back on how great their new media is. NEW Media? It's the same old shit, the equal of boy bands and action flicks and stupid game shows in A NEW FORMAT. It's All Shit! Merde! Merde! Merde! You're not fucking Jack Kerouac, you're just some bozos with DSL connections and a penchant for buying soon-to-be-obsolete gadgets and appearing in pretentious periodicals, you superficial gits.

BLOGMA 2001 calls all true webloggers to rise up and overthrow the bourgeoisie. BLOGMA 2001 requires that the nascent culture of the celebrity blogger be utterly smashed before there is nothing else. BLOGMA 2001 demands a return to entries with good content and good links, not just endorsements of the latest PalmPilot. BLOGMA 2001 insists that the standard of weblogging return to the halcyon days of 1999.

And newbie bloggers, just because you might have only picked this up recently, that does not mean you can't be part of the revolution. Of course you can. There is a place for anyone who gives a damn. So give a damn, and do not fall to the temptation of linking to these parasites. They'll take your hits, oh yes, but don't expect them to return them because they are scum. Yes, write about how you feel and what you've been experiencing and your response to the world around you. Don't be afraid of content. Don't be afraid to comment on what everyone else is talking about. Don't be afraid to link to what you like. Don't be afraid to share your stories or your opinions or your jokes or your friends. But don't ever take the view that just because you aren't on the A-list you don't matter. Of course you matter. If you do it well, people will notice.

After the elite are ripped down from their pedestals, we will issue Missive Two.

24

Blogma 2001
Missive Two: Further Matters;
and Some Clarifications

BLOGMA 2001 Committee
November 18, 2000

THE REACTION IN THE DAYS SINCE THE PUBLICATION OF OUR FIRST missive has been explosive, to say the least. Though much of it has been well intended, some people have misconstrued our aims, and in that we have not been entirely without fault. We are brilliant, but we are not perfect. We aim to clear up a few things in this missive.

Firstly: To those who say that we are merely attempting to unseat the existing hierarchy in order to replace it with another populated by our own good selves; you are absolutely correct. How else can we propagate the memes of virtuous and pure weblogging? Of course we intend to place ourselves at the top of the hierarchy. However, you will barely notice our leadership; after we cleanse the scene of the despicable infidels, our methods will become benign and benevolent: a nudge there, a tap here, a violently bloody pogrom of draconian measures every now and again just to keep everyone on their toes.

Secondly: To those who say we have not strictly followed the example of the Dogma 95 manifesto with regards to setting up guidelines for weblogging with the attendant Vow of Purity. We did have a go at this, but the Rules Subcommittee responsible for formulating those guidelines had a nine-hour marathon session debating whether the use of Blogger should be proscribed, and in the end we had to summarily execute the whole bloody lot of them because the main point of contention was over whether Megnut was bourgeois, which would impact on whether Pyra was a good firm with good people, or just another of these dot-coms evicting all the freaks from San Francisco. Someone misheard the chairman and interjected that Meg was indeed "gorgeous" with her bizarre hair and all. In a tense environment, this contentious remark sparked a heated and at times physical argument over the politics of beauty and personal identity, whereupon we had to send the dogs in. So the set of guidelines was never completed. Tell you what, as some of you are such world-wise digerati geniuses, why don't you send your suggestions in. This will save us having to appoint another subcommittee, which would potentially send another five delegates to their doom and give us another bloody mess to clean up. Let it not be said that we are without mercy.

Thirdly: To people using the American high school as a metaphor for the social dynamic of the scene, grow up. With these institutions fostering a climate of anti-intellectualism in a society obsessed with guns, death, sexual repression and the resulting frustration, it is no accident that every now and again the oppressed will go berko and mow their oppressors down in a hail of gunfire. What that has to do with weblogging we have no idea.

Fourthly: To people describing us as hypocrites. We know.

Missive Three will be concerned with the Great Satan that is Jakob Nielsen.

Weblogging: Lessons Learned

Kulesh Shanmugasundaram

November 1, 1999

Nothing in the Name

Don't hit your head on the wall to name a weblog. Choosing a random name is fine; however, I wouldn't recommend pneumonoultramicroscopicsilicovolcanoconiosis for a name. Choose an easy to remember name even if it doesn't make any sense.

Content Is Everything

Content is everything. Great contents make great weblogs. Be original, be unique. Always comment on links you provide. Tell the readers what to expect and what you think about it. Be observant, that is one of the best ways to find great contents. You are unique just like everyone else. You might see a different perspective altogether. Regular updates are mandatory, daily updates are not.

Kiss That Design Goodbye

Good design is . . . well just good. Keep the weblog compatible across browsers. It's recommended not to use Flash or other plug-ins. One of the reasons why design is not important is people visit your weblog regularly. Even if you have a mind blowing design they will eventually get used to it. On the other hand, people should be able to read your weblog from anywhere. Hey, sometimes I read weblogs with Lynx, really.

Don't Be an Addict

Read weblogs regularly, just don't get addicted to one or two weblogs. It's always better to have a broad view. By reading one or two weblogs very often you might be influenced by the views of those weblogs. Remember it's your views that count.

10 Million vs. 10

Having 10 million hits is not the game plan. Having 10 regular readers is a home run.

Simple Is Success

Readers come from a variety of backgrounds. Write to the point, be simple and short. Excessive English is just not going to help. I don't want to spend two minutes flipping through a dictionary. Usually I spend a minute or two on a weblog to see if there is anything new and interesting. You probably have 30 to 45 seconds to get a user's attention. If you have to write long, separate them from the daily log.

Sights, Sounds & Style

Having a unique style is important. Having a consistent style in letter formatting helps in getting readers' attention to a specific area. Having a unique style of writing helps in getting regular readers. Be funny if that's your thing or be professional; just don't be boring. No, you don't need to follow the *Chicago Manual of Style*.

Be Nice to Bloggers

Be polite when you comment on others. Remember everyone is entitled to their opinion and you should respect that. If you don't like something, say it as politely as you can. If you like something, do appreciate it, and if you want to add something, go ahead. Just be nice. Don't be a wise ass. Also a good point to remember is that webloggers are not some Internet junkies. There are very highly respected individuals in this elite community, such as Internet pioneers, inventors, professors, excellent designers, programmers, etc. They know what they are doing and they are damn good at what they do.

Avoid Ass-kissing

Avoid ass-kissing at all cost. Initially you will not get lots of traffic; eventually you will, depending on the contents. Just praising a highly trafficked weblog is not going to help; instead it may backfire on you. Remember the 10 million vs. 10 rule.

Anonymous Is Okay

Nobody wants to know who you are or what you do as long as you have something interesting in the weblog. So being anonymous is okay. Some readers may find it interesting to figure out an identity for you. If you are being anonymous give some hints about you from time to time. "I am a fat boy!"

26

The Libera Manifesto

Chris Pirillo
March 16, 2001

The Other Side of Your Screen

libera: (Latin) free, independent, unrestricted

As the provider of a four-year standing free service, I thought it was time someone shared these basic truths with the rest of the world. Too often, we fall victim to gross misconceptions. The Libera Manifesto intends to speak for those who provide something online for free. If you believe in this manifesto, join the rest of us[1] by signing below, using this graphic to link to it on your website, and emailing the URL to a friend.

This was published to expose a silent perspective—one which most Internet users cannot see outright. These are not definitive policies, merely concepts to which most "freebie" providers adhere. You can love us or spite us, but remember: without us, you'd have to pay for everything.

Consider the following a tribute to those who have supported us in the past; we are forever in your debt. This is very much a living piece; I am open to adding new principles as the community sees fit. If there's enough interest, we'll add resources for the Liberati (mailing list, forums, etc.). Check back often.

Our Manifesto was not compiled to ostracize, single out, offend, or hurt anybody; if it truly upsets you, please read through it a few more times. DO NOT FEEL GUILTY—feel empowered.

The Libera Manifesto version 1.0

1. Our time is worth something, too.
2. There is such a thing as a free lunch, but don't forget to tip your waiter.
3. We love to create without charging for our work.
4. Feedback keeps us going.
5. Sponsors are not beating down our doors.
6. All take and no give only works for a little while.
7. If you don't like something, do it yourself.
8. Don't expect us to ask for nothing in return.
9. We are human.
10. Half the world disagrees with us. The other half disagrees.
11. Five years ago, we were different people.
12. Five years ago, the Internet was a different place.
13. If you can help, please do.
14. Don't expect us to do everything, all the time, anytime you want us to do it for you.
15. We love you.
16. Free is not always free.
17. Think before you complain.
18. We don't waste time; we give it to you.
19. Without you, we'd be nothing.
20. It just looks easy.
21. Which do you value more: our services or an Extra Value Meal?
22. When you "cheat" the system, it hurts the giver more than it helps the taker.

23. Spare time?
24. Affiliate programs pay jack squat.
25. We don't whine, we ask politely.
26. Bandwidth is not free.
27. Nobody is forcing you to use our stuff.
28. Negative feedback is not the same as constructive criticism.
29. You'd be surprised at how much a digital "pat on the back" would brighten our day.
30. We don't know everything.
31. We need your respect and understanding.
32. We still love you.
33. Most of us operate without a budget.
34. If you like us, tell a friend.
35. If you hate us, tell us why.
36. Some of us are too humble to ask you to do something for us.
37. Weekends do not exist.
38. We made a choice to do this, but we also have the right to change our minds.
39. You don't get what you pay for.
40. Don't count on someone else to pick up the slack.
41. Personal life?
42. We want to give you more.
43. Our service is part of our spirit.
44. We respect your advice, but can't always follow it.
45. Assume nothing.
46. Our business plan consists of one goal: be here tomorrow.
47. If we ever develop a "pay for" option, we'll have good reason to do so.
48. Even if we do develop a "pay for" option, you don't have to buy it.

49. We want to connect with people, not machines.
50. Integrity means more to us than our bottom line.
51. Don't expect us to bash Company X.
52. Don't expect us to praise Company X.
53. The term "IPO" is not in our vocabulary.
54. If we have a published set of instructions or frequently asked questions, please read it.
55. Sleep is a luxury.
56. Most of us seek recognition, not fame.
57. Offer suggestions, but never tell us how to do our job.
58. Our character is sometimes the only thing we can count on; don't question it.
59. Go ahead and call us "sellouts." You're wrong.
60. Take us for granted and soon there will be nothing left to take.
61. Making money is not always our goal.
62. We remember those who help us.
63. We remember those who do NOT help us.
64. Most of us don't have a "Director of Marketing." (WG²)
65. We like free stuff, too.
66. Without us, you'd have to pay for everything.
67. The advertising market has changed; we have struggled to remain the same.
68. There's nothing wrong with reciprocation.
69. This is a full-time job, whether we have another one or not.
70. Ignore us and we'll go away.
71. If we can't afford to continue, we can't afford to continue.
72. Lurking is fine—just let us know that we're helping you at some point.
73. Don't confuse personality with ego.
74. Most of us ride on the Cluetrain.
75. Opinions aren't wrong.
76. We'll always love you.

The Inspiration

I decided to start this list when I heard that shyfonts.com closed due to the following reasons. I knew he wasn't alone:

> I just wasn't receiving that much support from my users. Everybody kept downloading all of the fonts, but never supported the site. I'd get almost 2,000 hits a day and no one would really click an ad or buy one of our shirts (only one person ever bought a shirt). What made it worse, with the traffic I received, hardly anybody ever sent me an email just to say thanks. I just couldn't afford to keep the site up anymore. It really sucks too, because I've spent a lot of time and effort on ShyFonts.

We really don't ask for that much.

27

Ten Tips for
Building a Bionic Weblog

Metascene
September 13, 2000

1. Are you sure you want to do this?

Posting a weblog or any kind of personal webpage should be fun. If you are not having a good time, why bother? If you are doing this for reasons other than personal satisfaction, chances are you will be disappointed. If you're not having fun putting it together, how can you expect other folks to have a good time reading it?

2. Take a good look around at what everyone else is doing and then DO SOMETHING ELSE.

Find a niche or a voice or an angle, something to differentiate yourself from the crowd. For example, why post links to stuff that has already been linked EVERYWHERE ELSE? In order to be the same? How exciting! A sure-fire way to attract legions of readers and die-hard fans—by doing exactly what everyone else is doing!

I'm not saying that you should never dabble in meme-spreading, but be selective and try to add your own spin to the thing.

Take chances.

(*Ed. Note: Only at tip #2 and already we have a problem! For while I'm telling you to be "different" and "original," it seems that I'm like the 57th weblogger to write about weblogging. To be honest, I was a bit skeptical of the essays posted on the Weblog Madness[1] resource page, but having just sampled a few of them, I see that there is some good advice being dispensed there.*)

3. Fuck the numbers.

Fuck traffic, fuck hits, fuck ratings. It's all hogwash.

Many of the best sites out there are under-read, under-rated or undiscovered. Use your "poor standing" as motivation to KICK SOME ASS. Show those fuckers what they are missing out on. Post unique, original stuff and people will notice you. Until then, let spite be your best friend, your muse, your *raison d'être*. Walk around with a big ol' chip on your shoulder 'cause you're doing a bang-up job, even if nobody has noticed. Be proud to be a hip, underground weblog, read only by a few in the know. I would not trade a handful of readers I respect and like for 10,000 hits a day from people just following the herd.

Now if it were 50,000 a day, that might be something different, but until then . . .

I would rather have an original, not so well-known blog that I was having fun with and could be proud of than to have a Big Fat Famous Weblog that was posting crap. Wouldn't you? Obscurity is not something to be sought after but it does offer some advantages. Use them while you can.

(*Ed. Note: If you are a Big Famous Brand Name Weblog, I am not talking about you. I'm talking about the other Big Famous Brand Name Weblogs. Just so long as we're clear about that.*)

4. Getting noticed.

That being said, if you want to have more than just a few friends and co-workers reading your blog (mainly out of sympathy I assure you), you have to give some love to get some love. Every now and then, post links to some of the weblogs you most enjoy. Send fan mail to bloggers you admire. And by fan mail, I don't mean something lame like, "Would you link me on your huge stupid ass page of weblog links?"

Try something like, "Hey. I really like what you're doing. I too have a weblog. Maybe sometime when you get a chance you could check it out." If you are really daring, maybe you don't ask them to read your crap, but just include a subtle little link in the signature to pique their interest.

Also, when sending email, try to be funny and demonstrate some familiarity with what they are doing. Flattery doesn't hurt either, but be sincere. Try to figure out what it is you like about their style.

You do have a style, right? If you're not sure, you'd better check it out. Style helps. My personal style is "corny and pretentious; a profound arrogance hiding behind a fig leaf of false modesty; spineless; half-smart."

5. Do not expect anything in return for linking to someone.

Can we please just stop this nonsense right now? If the Weblog Spirit moves you to mention on your blog that such and such linked you, then go ahead. After all, it's your freaking blog and you should post whatever you like. But I think it's best not to expect anything in return. Often I have too much respect for a weblog that has linked me to post a reciprocal link. Doing so cheapens the whole thing, no? Allow the person who linked you to be generous.

In turn, maybe you will consider linking to someone else, hopefully a weblog that is under-read or not well known.

If you are generous, others will be generous towards you.

Linking to another weblog to get their attention = Good

Linking to another weblog in the expectation of getting linked back = Pathetic

I mean, do you really want someone to link to you just because you linked to them first? We should all have to earn our links. Otherwise, this whole thing just becomes an embarassment.

6. More on getting noticed.

Once in a while it may be a good idea to post some original content that you've created. I think you will find that people will be very generous in their praise for whatever crap you come up with. I mean, did you see that half-assed piece on the MTV awards I posted? You did? SEE! Some people even said nice things about it. But I don't hold that against them.

Maybe they thought it was funny. Maybe they were just being nice. There's nothing wrong with being nice and truth be told, I will look for ways to be nice in return, hopefully without being too obvious.

7. Mix it up a little.

Every now and then check to make sure your schtick isn't getting stale. Avoid formulas. If you find you are only linking to *Salon* or *Wired* or newspaper articles, try to include some other kinds of links. If I have to explain what I mean by "other kinds of links" then maybe you should consider doing something other than a weblog.

Of course, *Salon* and *Wired* are both fine publications.

8. Confidence is sexy.

Have some opinions. Have a spine. Don't be afraid to have your own opinions, no matter how unpopular you think they might be; we may surprise you. Avoid easy targets. Avoid the obvious. Avoid cheap shots. Don't be afraid to admit what you like.

That being said, don't be an asshole. Arrogance is just plain ugly. Now it may seem that I break this "don't be a conceited asshole" rule all the time, but that's only because I am one charming and brilliant motherfucker. And don't you forget it. Ever.

9. See Tip #3.

Seriously. Don't get all caught up in it. If the numbers make you feel good, fine. If they gnaw at you night and day and are threatening to make you a bitter person, please, leave it alone.

Do I find the ratings interesting and a good place to check out other weblogs? Yes. Do I take it seriously? Please.

(*Special Metascene Insider Bonus Tip! If you get a chance to take the Beebo guy out to dinner, by all means, do so.*)

10. Some general suggestions.

- Play reporter once in a while. Research under-reported stories and do some leg work for your readers. Find an angle that no one, including mainstream press, has reported on.
- Link to original sources of infomation. Also, share your sources, especially if they are other weblogs. You may want to keep a few cheat sheets to yourself, but let us in on a few good ones you've found.
- Resist the urge to post a blurb about every time you get up from your desk to go to the bathroom or to get a soda.

Please. You must be strong for all of us. If, however, while you are in the bathroom some insane person starts barking at you, then you may feel free to post something about that.

- Once in a while remind yourself that just because it happenned to you does not necessarily make it interesting.
- People like links about monkeys, robots, sexual perversion, and any combination thereof. Well, at least I do. I cannot stress this point enough. More robot monkey sex links please.
- Once in a while remind yourself that you are not only as good as your last update. There will be time enough . . .
- Link to independent type things, i.e., personal pages, zines, sites a bit off the beaten path. I'm not saying not to post to well-known national publications and such, but mix it up once in a while. Support independent media—if you don't, who will?
- Quality, not quantity is job one. (Unless you're an auto maker and you can find a way to cut some corners on manufacturing tires.) Sometimes, if you post a billion links, some of the good ones that maybe you worked hard to find, will get lost in the clutter. Don't shoot yourself in the foot by burying the link. (Unless it's out of spite, in which case you're on your trip and don't need any of this advice anyway.) If you want people to click on the links, you have to do a little selling. I'm lazy so I use a lot of pull-quotes but I try to mix it up some.
- Also, posting good entries is more important than posting every friggin day. This is not to say you shouldn't post every day, just that you don't have to. That being said, if you know you will be taking an extended leave of absence, it's nice to let your readers know.

- There is no accounting for taste. These are just some random thoughts about some qualities I like in a weblog. There are many fine weblogs that specialize in stuff I know nothing about or am not that interested in or that have taken another approach to weblogging. Which is fine. Even if I don't read those logs everyday, I like to check in every now and then just to see what's up.

11. Break some rules.

28

Put the Keyboard Down and Back Away from the Weblog

Neale Talbot

March 28, 2000

THAT'S RIGHT. YOU HEARD ME.

Get yer[1] stinking 3000+[2] hands away from my posts.

You wanna write a journal, go ahead. You wanna create content, fine by me. But if you and yer redneck communist pals come round here and start messing with the blogs, there's gonna be hell and high water.

Why?

Coz I like 'em Sharp'n'pointed'n'bitter.[3]

Coz I like 'em Short'n'sweet'n'sour.[4]

Coz I like catching up on what's hot,[5] and what's happening,[6] and doing it in between the drudgery and smudgery of work.

Watcha gotta fear from the blogs?[7] Sure they share similar elements to the journal[8] world, but that don't mean one will eat the other. Distinct places. Distinct genres. You say[9] it's the same old shit in the same old package. Well I say it's a lot less shit in a much smaller package. And where I come from, the less shit[10] the better. Maybe it's different where you are.

Maybe I don't wanna see fantastic design from a designer or fantastic writing from a writer every single day. Maybe I wanna

157

get a sense of the opinions[11] of those around me, and the things they're interested in, not their fucking life story.[12]

The last thing I need is ten 500-word essays about the repercussions of Napster[13] being banned by universities, or Microbloodysoft[14] delaying the launch of its next crappy product. I need 15 separate dissertations on the meaning of *Wired's*[15] stupid-as-fuck redesign like I need a hole in the head.

If I were to read 3000+ words from the 20+ weblogs I read each day, I'd be wading through a fucking novel every morning. I'd have to print them out and take them to bed with me. I could then feed the fireplace with their stilted prose and repetitive bullshit. No-thank-you.

They're different styles for different audiences about different things. If you're to employ the same styles to both, you'd have something like this:

Blog Style Journal

Freudian slip last night. Meant to ask wife to pass the salt. Instead said, "Fuck off bitch, you're ruining my life."

Journal Style Blog

Hackers got hold of Bill Gates's credit card.[16] I remember once when I had my wallet stolen. I was on my honeymoon, and had just been wandering through a cinema when it happened. I was carrying my coat through a crowd and didn't notice anything, even though some dumb fuck's nimble fingers ran their way between the folds of my clothes, and made off with my wallet. I didn't realize until my wife and I decided to go to a restaurant for dinner, and yadda yadda yadda . . .

I'm not sure which one is worse.

So what's the difference between the blog and the journal?

The blog points outward. The journal points inward. The blog talks about the objective world. The journal talks about the subjective world. Yes, there is overlap.[17] Yes, there is cross-pollination.[18] But for the most part, weblogs talk about things that happen regardless of the writer's existence. The subject matter of journals would not be there if the writers didn't exist.

Are you listening? Are you getting it?

The journal needs to be involved and intricate and well written as the subject matter demands it. The blog can be short and wicked because the subject matter demands nothing.

So leave yer 3000+ words at the door, buddy, because it doesn't work for this medium.

You can use the blogging[19] tools[20] to write your journal, but that don't make it a blog.

You can add as many links as you want, but that don't make it a blog.

You can register myfuckingweblog.weblog.com[21] if you want, but if you start writing 3000+ words about your personal life, it ain't gonna give it one ounce of blog cred.

You understand?

PART FIVE

Weblogs vs. Traditional Journalism

29

Blogging as a Form of Journalism: Weblogs Offer a Vital, Creative Outlet for Alternative Voices

J. D. Lasica

May 24, 2001

BACK AROUND 1993, IN THE WEB'S NEOLITHIC DAYS, STARRY-EYED Net denizens waxed poetic about a million websites blooming and supplanting the mainstream media as a source of news, information and insight.

Then reality set in and those individual voices became lost in the ether as a million businesses lumbered onto the cyberspace stage, newspapers clumsily grasped at viable online business models, and a handful of giant corporations made the Web safe for snoozing.

But a funny thing happened on the way to the Web's irrelevance: the blogging phenomenon, a grassroots movement that may sow the seeds for new forms of journalism, public discourse, interactivity and online community.

While no one is really sure where this is all heading, my hunch is that blogging represents Ground Zero of the personal webcasting revolution. Weblogging will drive a powerful new form of amateur journalism as millions of Net users—young people especially—take on the role of columnist, reporter, analyst, and publisher while fashioning their own personal broadcasting networks. It won't happen overnight, and we're now seeing only version 1.0, but just wait a few years when broadband and multimedia arrive in a big way.

For the uninitiated, a blog consists of a running commentary with pointers to other sites. Some, like Librarian.net,[1] Jim Romenesko's Media News,[2] or Steve Outing's E-Media Tidbits,[3] cover entire industries by providing quick bursts of news with links to full stories. But most blogs are simply rolling personal journals—ongoing links-laden riffs on a favorite subject.

For more on the basics of blogs, see the good backgrounders provided by *OJR* columnist Ken Layne[4] and by Glenn Fleishman in the *Seattle Times*.[5]

I spoke this month with six journalists or writers who publish weblogs and asked for their take on the phenomenon and its significance for journalism. Three appear below and three will appear next week.

Paul Andrews[6]

Andrews, who now lives in San Francisco, was technology columnist for the *Seattle Times* before taking an early buyout. He co-authored the book *Gates* (Doubleday, 1993) and wrote *How the Web Was Won*[7] (Broadway Books, 1999), about Microsoft's embrace of the Internet. He began his weblog in November.

Weblogs come in all shapes and flavors, and Andrews has sampled plenty of them. "Some are tech-based, some are glorified dating services, some are nothing but a collection of links. The ones I like the most give something personal as well," he says.

Not everyone who keeps a journal is a journalist, he points out, and "you can write on the Web about your work and life without being a journalist." But professional journalists too often dismiss those who don't work for traditional media, he says, when the truth is that the most vital and moral dispatches on the Web are being created by amateurs.

"It's the role of institutional media to act as gatekeepers," he says, "but what you have in print publishing today is a consolidation that's inimical to the diversity that exists in everyday life. With the rise of the Internet, people don't need to be bounded by those traditional filters anymore."

The Net opens up the spigots for those who want to take on the mantle of journalist. "The Web gives voice to a lot of alternative points of view," Andrews says. "Anyone connected with the WTO protests in Seattle and Quebec City knows that the protestors' viewpoints were either ignored or misrepresented by the radio, TV and newspaper coverage. The commentary was almost willfully ignorant. How silly, how arrogant that alternative voices were not allowed to be heard. I always thought the role of the journalist is to ensure that the voice of the people should be exposed.

"Now, thankfully, the protesters who want to get their story out can bypass the media by using live audio or a webcam to offer raw feeds during a live protest or forum. If you're a guy with a video recorder filming an event in a certain neighborhood and streaming it on the Internet and reporting it on your weblog, you're practicing a straightforward kind of amateur journalism."

Andrews thinks weblogs and other forms of online journalism are on the rise in part because of the rapid decline in the credibility of big media. "I think the Web is actually becoming more credible while established media are losing ground," he says. "And name me the last five serious efforts at public interest journalism by institutionalized media."

Andrews doubts that we'll see many journalists at traditional media companies launch their own personal weblogs. (*New Re-*

public columnist Andrew Sullivan[8] is one exception.) "I think newspapers still look askance at the Web and they don't want their reporters online even on their own time," he says.

Part of the reason for the upsurge in blogging at sites like weblogger.com[9] and blogger.com[10] is that the tools for self-publishing have become far easier and more automated. "When the first browsers were invented, you still had to know how to script," Andrews says. "Now you've got templates and applications and free server space so that all the nuts and bolts are taken care of for you and all you have to do is concentrate on the writing."

Andrews lays out a sort of manifesto for journalism blogging in a disquisition called Who Are Your Gatekeepers?[11] In it he gives a fascinating historical survey of the role played by publishers of first-person journals, noting that Columbus' ship log with his personal ruminations became the hot news publication of its day, and that the first newspaper in America was shut down by colonial authorities for printing unsanctioned gossip about the king of France's sex life and a local suicide.

Writes Andrews: "A new style of journalism, based on a 'raw feed' directly from the source, is emerging. Journalists testing the new waters are . . . bound to wreak havoc on institutionalized media. . . . Where the weblog changes the nature of 'news' is in the migration of information from the personal to the public. . . . Hit the 'post' button and any personal writing becomes published writing. . . . As a thousand flowers bloom, the Web's garden of information becomes more diverse, enlightening and transformative than anything the traditional paper-based print world can provide."

Since writing that several weeks ago, Andrews has dialed back his rhetorical flourishes a notch. "I'm a little more measured today," he says. "The dot-com implosion and the vision for the Internet has a lot of us going through a reassessment. It's also been sobering to realize what a demanding form of expression weblogging is. On the whole it'll be a slower uptick than I predicted earlier. But my kids and their kids live on the Internet, and as their world evolves it will be much more of an electronically published world."

Does he still think weblogs will bring about a new form of journalism?

"That's the key question," he says. "I don't know. If the tools become more sophisticated, if bots can point you to other bloggers whose ideas match criteria you've set up, then I think we'll evolve to a different kind of journalism. Right now it's still too hard to make those connections. But I'm still hopeful. We're getting there."

Deborah Branscum[12]

Branscum, based in Berkeley, Calif., is a contributing editor to *Newsweek* who wrote a feature on blogging[13] for the magazine's March 5 issue. She is also a contributor to *Fortune.com*, *Macworld*, *Wired*, *PC World* and other publications. She began her weblog in December.

"I began doing a weblog for a patently self-serving reason: to promote my not-yet-world-famous conference[14] for technology and PR executives," Branscum says. "A weblog gives me a forum where I can bitch bluntly about the many failings of media PR. But it's become just addictive and incredibly fun to do."

Branscum ticks off four cool things about weblogs:

Creative freedom. Part of a blog's allure is its unmediated quality. "For a working journalist, there's no luxury like the luxury of the unedited essay," she says. "I've been an editor longer than I've been a writer, and I know the value that an editor brings to your copy. Even so, there's an enormous freedom in being able to pre-

sent yourself precisely as you want to, however sloppily or irra-
tionally or erratically. I don't have an editor to pitch the story to,
or a copy editor who decides he's not happy with my syntax . . .
You think it, you write it, you put it out to the world."

Instantaneity. "Even when you're writing for a weekly magazine, it seems like it takes forever to see your work in print,"
Branscum says. "With a weblog, you hit the send key and it's out
there. It's the perfect disposable journalism for our age."

Interactivity. "It's a kick to get feedback from people you've
never heard of who stumble on your weblog," she says. Branscum estimates that 30 readers might surf her blog on a slow day
and 900 might read it on a busy day, with pointers from other
sites and other bloggers often driving traffic to archived material.

Lack of marketing constraints. "The people who are interested in
your perspective find you, instead of you having to find a publication that reflects their interests," she says. "You don't have to necessarily tailor your work for a certain readership or demographic."

Like most bloggers, Branscum updates her weblog sporadi-
cally, averaging twice a week. She blogs mostly about media matters, from the state of entertainment journalism[15] to a rant on
rude reporters.[16]

Does Branscum think we're slouching toward some new form
of journalism? "I'm not quite willing to go there," she says, "but I
do think it's an interesting question for PR folks and the people
who have to deal with webloggers. My attitude is, if you haven't
established your credibility by writing for any major publications, it's not written down anywhere that people have to answer
your questions. So far, the weblogs I've seen tend to be less about
actual reporting and more about analysis and punditry and opinionated commentary."

For now, independent journalists will continue to devote their
time and energy to publications that pay, Branscum says. "Unless

someone figures out a way to pay journalists for our weblogs, my best efforts will go to *Fortune.com* and *Newsweek*. For now, weblogs are a fabulous exercise in self-indulgence because you're writing for yourself."

Glenn Fleishman[17]

Fleishman, based in Seattle, is a free-lance reporter for the *New York Times*, *Wired*, and *Fortune* and a computer columnist for the *Seattle Times*. He began writing a weblog on technology and his personal life in November.

"Blogging was this phenomenon that I thought of as not very interesting for a long while," recalls Fleishman, a freelancer since 1994. "When the Guild at the *Seattle Times* went on strike[18] last November, I came across Paul Andrews' weblog and discovered how easy it was to set up the tools. I decided to try it out."

Fleishman came to the same conclusion as Branscum: that weblogs are taken more seriously than a static webpage. "It's this gem, this nut, that people interact with differently," Fleishman says. "A weblog gives off a patina of credibility and authoritativeness that you don't find in other corners of the Web."

The medium seemed well-suited to Fleishman, a self-described "pretty opinionated guy." His weblog tends to focus on technology issues like low-speed wireless networks or his six-month stint at Amazon.com.[19] His goal is to parlay his blog into a "dead-tree job" as a full-time columnist for a print publication.

Fleishman found that he could use his weblog to report or discuss issues that fell outside the scope of an article he was writing for a print publication. "Issues kept coming up in my reporting that I couldn't include in my report, often because I was expressing an opinion and my story wasn't an analysis or how-to piece," he says. His weblog gave him a forum to publish relevant reporting that would have remained buried in his notebook.

Another advantage of weblogs is that you're not completely at the mercy of big media. Fleishman cites the example of Dave Winer, a software entrepreneur whom John Markoff interviewed for an article in the *New York Times* last month. "Dave said the article gave an inaccurate interpretation of what he had to say. He gave his own account[20] on his site to clarify his position."

For journalists, Fleishman says, weblogs offer one overriding appeal: here's a media form that lets you write at any length about any issue you care deeply about. "As a reporter, it's nice to be able to present an informed conclusion, based on your own experience, without having to go to the requisite two dozen so-called expert analysts who cancel each other out," he says. "You're the only one who's standing behind this opinion."

Fleishman doesn't buy into the standard blogger mantra that unmediated writing is superior to copy that has passed through the editorial sausage factory. He finds blogging neither superior nor inferior to traditional journalism—just infinitely fascinating. "One of the most interesting things about blogs is how often they've made me change my mind about issues," he says. "There's something about the medium that lets people share opinions in a less judgmental way than when you interact with people in the real world."

That's what seems to resonate with bloggers: not the publication of a first-person journal but the chain of interaction it often ignites. Says Fleishman: "Someone spots an article or commentary you've posted, which triggers a blog entry, which triggers further responses, and before you know it your blog becomes part of an interactive discussion in this obscure backwater of the Web that's being read and cited by thousands of people. It's pretty amazing."

Weblogs:
A New Source of News

J. D. Lasica
May 31, 2001

WILL WEBLOGS DISPLACE ESTABLISHED MEDIA ORGANIZATIONS AS A source of news, information, and opinion? Not in this lifetime. But they will continue to make inroads as a supplement to traditional news sources.

As Doc Searls, one of the deep thinkers in the blog movement, says: "It's a matter of 'and' logic, not 'or' logic. Weblogs will inform old media. They will increasingly be a source of information that traditional media will rely on."

The first weblog has generally been ascribed to Dave Winer (interviewed below) in 1997. Blogs began taking off in 1999 with the launch of sites like Blogger,[1] Weblogger,[2] and LiveJournal,[3] which made self-publishing painless for the masses. While tens of thousands of blogs have blossomed, mainstream media have only recently shown a glimmer of interest in the form.

That's hardly surprising. Weblogs are the anti-newspaper in some ways. Where the editorial process can filter out errors and polish a piece of copy to a fine sheen, too often the machinery turns even the best prose limp, lifeless, sterile, and homogenized. A huge part of blogs' appeal lies in their unmediated quality. Blogs tend to be impressionistic, telegraphic, raw, honest, individualistic, highly opinionated and passionate, often striking an emotional chord.

Sometimes they veer toward immediacy and conjecture at the expense of accuracy and thoughtful reflection. But the best news blogs offer a personal prism that combines pointers to trusted sources of information with a subjective, passion-based journalism. If nothing else, weblogs are about personal publishing—people sharing what's in their gut and backing it up with facts or persuasion.

The serendipity factor looms large. Weblog writing may not often sparkle but it often surprises. Blogs unearth the strange, the quirky, the interesting nugget that would have remained hidden. As more people take up weblogging and more of us come to rely on blogs to help us shape our own personal media universe, media organizations would do well to incorporate them into their websites as an important new addition to the journalistic toolkit.

Here's a sampling of a few publications featuring weblogs:

- Dan Gillmor of the *San Jose Mercury News* has been publishing a daily weblog[4] on the paper's SiliconValley.com site for more than 18 months.
- Gael Fashingbauer Cooper, a staffer with the *Minneapolis Star Tribune*, tackles subjects like genealogy, webcams, and other topics of reader interest in a weekly weblog[5] launched in February 2000 that recently began appearing in the print newspaper as well.
- Aaron Barnhart, television columnist for the *Kansas City Star*, publishes a weblog at TVBarn.com.[6]
- *Boston Globe* business reporter D. C. Denison recently began writing a tech-news weblog.[7]
- Derek Willis writes a weblog called The Scoop[8] for *Congressional Quarterly* and publishes another on his personal site.[9]

- Suzanne Lainson writes a blog about the Colorado tech scene, written in the style of a society columnist, for Courtney Pulitzer's *The Cyber Scene*.[10] "It turns out it has been a much more enjoyable experience than I had ever imagined," Lainson says by email. "I can write about people, companies, and events that wouldn't be considered newsworthy in a traditional sense. While I do incorporate serious reporting, I offer considerable commentary—a good chunk of it done tongue in cheek."
- Kathy Shaidle, a religion columnist for the *Toronto Star*, publishes the Relapsed Catholic Weblog.[11]
- *The Guardian* in the United Kingdom runs a good international-news weblog.[12]
- *OJR*'s long-running Spike Report[13] dishes up interesting factoids culled from online news publications. *Slate*'s Today's Papers[14] and Omnivore[15] cover similar blog-like turf.
- A number of alternative weeklies, such as the *San Francisco Bay Guardian*,[16] run weblogs.
- *The Christian Science Monitor*[17] plans to launch five topic-based blogs in about a month.

For a list of weblogs, Eatonweb[18] publishes lists broken down by category, while Yahoo lists dozens of popular sites[19] and Userland posts a running tally of its Top 100 sites.[20]

A word about the term *weblog*: we'll focus here on weblogs in the strict sense (where the content may run from journals and diaries to political screeds or travelogues, but the owner-publisher decides whether anyone else may post) rather than the more loosely defined genre that we'll call collective weblogs (community news sites such as Slashdot.org,[21] Kuro5hin.org,[22] Freerepublic.com[23]), which resemble forums but whose content relies heavily on links, short news snippets, essays, rants, and other blog-like features.

What does weblogging herald for journalism? Here are perspectives from three significant figures in the weblog movement:

Dan Gillmor[24]

Dan Gillmor, business columnist for the *Mercury News*, was the first mainstream journalist to author a weblog and have it published on a newspaper website. His eJournal runs daily, with excerpts published in the print edition.

Among his peers, Gillmor is considered the leading trailblazer of this new online journalism form, but he's typically modest about the mark he's made. "I'm still feeling my way into it, so I don't know the big answers here," he says. "Everyone's still kind of groping about where this is all heading, but weblogs have already become a significant phenomenon."

Regular readers of Gillmor's eJournal will recognize his commitment to user participation. "One of the things I'm sure about in journalism right now is that my readers know more than I do," he says. "To the extent that I can take advantage of that in a way that does something for everyone involved—that strikes me as pretty cool."

One fascinating aspect of Gillmor's weblog is how he lifts the veil from the workings of the journalism profession. "There have been occasions where I put up a note saying, 'I'm working on the following and here's what I think I know,' and the invitation is for the reader to either tell me I'm on the right track, I'm wrong, or at the very least help me find the missing pieces," he says. "That's a pretty interesting thing. Many thousands more people read my column in the newspaper than online, but I do hear back from a fair number of people from the weblog."

Gillmor rates the interactivity with readers as one of the most striking features about blogs. "I frequently hear from readers after a column, saying, 'That was interesting, but have you thought about this or that angle?' and often the answer is no, I hadn't, so the next time I return to the subject the missing piece makes its way into the article.

"I think journalists have to do that. I doubt there is a beat at any newspaper or publication or program where it is not the case that the readers collectively know more than the reporter," he says. "That shouldn't come as any great revelation. Anyone who's dealt with networks knows that the network knows more than the individual."

While other newspapers have been reluctant to embrace the form, Gillmor says, "In my case it helps that I'm working for people whose reaction is not fear and loathing but, wow, that sounds interesting, let's see how it works."

He encourages other publications to weigh the possible benefits of launching a weblog. "Journalists need to experiment more as a group—not with our core values or with things like getting it right, but with things like how we produce news. We're just going to get dull if we don't. We're in the midst of a change, where journalism is changing from a lecture into something that resembles something between a conversation and a seminar, and that's pretty exciting to me."

For journalists thinking of taking up weblogging, he cautions, "It's important to recognize that it takes a fair amount of work to do it right. Man, this is a beast that's hungry all the time."

Gillmor says professional journalism needs to make room for a new brand of amateur journalism that weblogs are helping to fashion. "No question, this is another kind of journalism. Technology has been leading us toward new ways of looking at things, and the idea of talented amateurs becoming part of the conversation is just the next logical step. It's the model of the pamphleteer journalist. Will the pamphleteer journalist become Gannett? No, but I don't think the pamphleteer wants to be Gannett."

He pauses and considers the future of blogging. "Let's see where it takes us," he says, "because clear as hell it's taking us somewhere interesting."

Doc Searls[25]

Doc Searls, based in Santa Barbara, California, is a veteran journalist, computer industry analyst, and senior editor for *Linux Journal*. He's best known as one of four authors of *The Cluetrain Manifesto*[26], a near-mythic essay that laid out 95 theses about the new reality of marketplaces in a networked world.

When Searls began his blog in November 1999, he found 9,000 search engine results for the term *weblog*. That number has since grown to more than 624,000.

He launched the weblog as an online counterpart to the book publication[27] of *Cluetrain*. "But in the course of that I discovered that weblogs are really personal, and as soon as you pluralize a voice, it loses some of its meaning," he says.

Searls believes that blogs offer the news media a means of "re-personalizing journalism," through their subject matter and by connecting journalists to other journalists' journals and to expert sources.

"That's what weblogs offer to journalism," he says. "Weblogs are personal journalism. For real journalists who aren't used to writing without a net, weblogs have a self-informing and self-correcting system built into it. When Dan Gillmor published an item whose source said it wasn't ready for public dissemination, Dan apologized and took it off his weblog, and that increased his stature. You can't do that with a regular paper—you'd get a re-traction instead."

One of the interesting hallmarks of a successful weblog is that it becomes an authoritative source of information based on com-munity endorsement. "People link to it, and those links increase the site's authority and raise its profile in as natural a way as pos-sible," Searls says. "So what we have is a marketplace in which we grant authority to those we trust to alter or author our own opinions. I let Dan supply me with many of my opinions because he's really good, not because his name is on the masthead of a print publication. Many of the weblogs I visit have no connection to the print world."

While many blogs get dozens or hundreds of visitors, Searls' site attracts thousands. "I partly don't want to care what the number is," he says. "I used to work in broadcasting, where everyone was obsessed by that. I don't want an audience. I feel I'm writing stuff that's part of a conversation. Conversations don't have audiences."

Searls says the media remain blind to the cultural and techno-logical changes that are overtaking traditional modes of commu-nication. "What's happening to every business is they're melting into the marketplace," he says. "It comes as a profound revela-tion to most in the first world when they discover that markets are a conversation. But in the third world that's a given—mar-kets are a bazaar, not a conveyor belt moving goods. They're about relationships and connoisseurship and social life—not something you can describe in accounting language. We forget that the price tag is only 125 years old. Before that, everything was negotiated.

"When we think about media or journalism," Searls says, "you have content that's loaded in a channel and delivered to a target group or demographic. That's just not applicable to the world of weblogs, where you go looking for interesting conversations, where you might run into soccer moms and students discussing Plato and a whole noisy marketplace speaking to itself. Journalism is going to have to get used to making room for lots of other people who are not journalists by training but who are just moved by whatever their nature happens to be."

Searls agrees with Gillmor (as do I) that many weblog authors are assuming the role of amateur journalists. "Just because you don't get paid for writing a blog doesn't mean you're any less authoritative," he says. (He writes more about what he calls "soft journalism"—the any-to-any system of talking and sharing rather than the traditional "hard journalism" model of writing that is distributed to the masses—in an essay[28] on his blog.)

Searls finds himself writing often in his blog about Linux, open-source software and the hacker community because those topics reflect his interests as senior editor at *Linux Journal*. "The blog serves as a kind of steam valve for me," he says. "I put stuff out there that I'm forming an opinion about, and another blogger starts arguing with me and giving me feedback, and I haven't even finished what I was posting!"

For mainstream journalists, Searls believes that weblogs will become an indispensable source of niche expertise. "For certain kinds of listings, farmer's markets, community events, movie reviews and the like, it's just a matter of time before traditional media give blogs their due. One loser in all this may be the traditional sources of authority—the analyst houses and think tanks and talking heads. They'll be quoted less because they're not part of the conversation. They won't be your sources of authority anymore. The weblog community is basically a whole bunch of expert witnesses who increase their expertise constantly through a sort of reputation engine."

Weblogs are already becoming an important source of news for readers. Searls says he found out that the author Douglas Adams died by reading the news[29] and an appreciation[30] on Dave Winer's blog. Says Searls: "I'd spent that day in the car listening to news stations in Santa Barbara and heard not a word about it—and he died in Santa Barbara! I picked up the local paper the next day and there wasn't a single word in there about his death. I was astonished."

Does Searls have any advice for aspiring bloggers? "You don't have to be a good writer. What matters is meaning. What you need is passion—a deep interest in a subject—and then all you have to do is say something interesting. For us readers, it's actually a bit like eavesdropping. Who do I want to drop in on unannounced?"

David Winer[31]

Winer, founder and CEO of Userland Software in Silicon Valley, has been credited as the first regular, widely followed blogger. He started Scripting News,[32] a weblog about technology, business and other weblogs, in early 1997, and began weblogging in early 1995 ("it wasn't called weblogging then," he notes).

Userland's software products power tens of thousands of weblogs. But for Winer, blogs are not just a publishing medium but a personal crusade that could foster a new brand of journalism. (He wrote about amateur journalism[33] on his DaveNet site.) His dream is to put a live Web server with easy-to-edit pages on every person's desktop, then connect them all in a robust network that feeds off itself and informs other media.

Winer might well be the godfather of the blogging movement, but a better term might be agent provocateur. His blog is peppered with musings, pointers to other sites, and Molotov cocktails that he lobs in the hope of sparking a lively debate. "We're all players in Uncle Dave's court," Searls says. Adds journalist-blogger Glenn Fleishman: "When you look at your stat sheet and see that your traffic spiked by 900 percent, you know that Dave has linked to you."

How great is Winer's influence among bloggers? When I asked Gillmor and Searls what spurred them to start a blog, both said the idea came from Winer.

For months Winer, a software developer and technology columnist for *Hotwired* in 1995–96, has denied that he's a journalist. But he now says, "I've finally resolved in my mind that I am a journalist. It's not how I earn my living, but I'd argue there's no less quality and integrity in being an amateur journalist. Maybe there's more integrity because my writing doesn't depend on a paycheck."

Winer stirred the pot April 17 with a provocative essay[34] on Web publishing that concluded: "Writers who work for others have less integrity to offer than those who do it for love." That drew retorts from Fleishman,[35] Deborah Branscum,[36] Searls,[37] and others, while Gillmor[38] also chimed in.

Winer often returns to the theme—familiar to any journalist who has wandered through Usenet or other back alleys of the Internet—that professional journalists are inherently compromised by the business interests and skewed editorial policies of their publications. (Winer would use language a tad stronger.)

Says Winer: "Some of the success I've had as a software developer is related to the fact that I'd had the ability to put my own story out there (on Scripting News), where I don't have to deal with cynical reporters who are interested only if it's being pushed by a big-name company or by editors who insist on dumbing down a concept because they think it's too complicated for their readers to handle. What happens if the casualty in that process is the truth?"

Winer says journalists are ignoring the serious work being done on weblogs, and online publishers should embrace the form. "Then they won't have to worry about dumbing it down, and multiple points of view will be able to get through."

He suggests that struggling sites like *Salon* begin broadening their content offerings by hosting user-created weblogs, creating a sort of farm system for essayists. "*Salon* could highlight the best ones on page one and invest time and effort in the ones that are inspiring and exceptional." He says online newspapers, too, should "go out and let anyone write for you. That's scary for professionals, who'll be put off by writers who may be just as talented but didn't have the patience to climb your stupid career ladder."

Winer says he checks in on about 200 weblogs on a regular basis. "You do it not so much to see what it gives you," he says. "It's more like checking in on a friend to see what's going on. It's like walking through a neighborhood, or reading columnists in a newspaper, even those you dislike because you enjoy the experience."

Winer has this advice for new bloggers: "If you have a story to tell—even if it's about some really mundane aspect of your life—you'll attract others who share your interest. Just don't set a goal of becoming the most popular person on the block. If you work too hard to be politically correct, if you go back and change your weblog because someone complained about something you posted, you'll wind up with writing that gets flat and boring. Self-censorship defeats the whole purpose of a weblog."

Indeed, Winer says his most gratifying moments come when he posts an entry without running the idea by his colleagues first. "It can be a very scary moment when you take a stand on something and you don't know if your argument holds together and you hit the send button and it's out there and you can't take it back. That's a moment that professional journalists may never experience in their careers, the feeling that it's just me, exposed to the world. That's a pretty powerful rush, the power to publish as an individual."

Blogged Down in the PR Machine: Publicists Diss Niche Queries for Now, Citing Time Constraints

Jordan Raphael
May 16, 2001

RELATIVELY SPEAKING, JOE CLARK WASN'T ASKING FOR MUCH: AN EMAIL interview with a manager or engineer at Apple Computer Inc. to discuss the company's OS X operating system. He wanted to explore how the platform's approach to localization issues could be applied to multilingual websites.

"So the piece you are working on right now regarding localization is for what publication?" emailed a staffer at Edelman Public Relations Worldwide, Apple's PR firm, on April 20.

Clark's response: "[I]t took 15 days to pose that question? The original message [stated it was] on the NUblog where the piece will appear. Hoping to hear back before May 4."

Clark can be forgiven for his annoyance; most journalists, especially at mid-level publications and smaller, have experienced similar frustration when publicists take days or weeks to reply to queries on time-sensitive stories, or sometimes don't reply at all.

But consider the harried, overworked PR rep. She's struggling to set up interviews for dozens of legitimate journalists from print, broadcast, and, yes, even online outlets, and suddenly she has to deal with someone claiming to be a writer for NUblog. What is a "NUblog," anyway?

Well, NUblog[1] is a weblog maintained by Clark. It's one among tens of thousands of individually produced sites containing personal musings, links, and other Net-based ephemera that have sprung up in recent years. Weblogs, known informally as blogs, can range in subject matter from light-hearted sincerity[2] to stark surreality,[3] tinged by the predilections and artistic inclinations of their authors.

NUblog belongs to a burgeoning subset of this community: blogs produced by journalists, sites such as AndrewSullivan.com,[4] Dan Gillmor's eJournal,[5] and Jim Romenesko's MediaNews.[6]

Many journalist-run blogs have small but dedicated followings of opinion leaders and influencers, the key people that PR companies are trying to target. In their niche-geared, serendipitous way, blogs reach a significant proportion of the Web's mindshare. In so doing, they may exert an influence rivaling that of traditional news outlets.

Yet, PR agencies are only now beginning to wake up to the importance of weblogs in the mediasphere, and many aren't sure how to deal with them. "The demands on PR people have gone through the roof because of the proliferation of online media," says Jerry Swerling, head of the public relations sequence at the USC Annenberg School for Communication. "What's lacking here is some kind of procedure or guidelines that tell corporate PR that a request is on the up and up."

The PR folks at Edelman and Apple apparently didn't consider Clark to be a legitimate journalist. After an increasingly hostile exchange with Clark, which is detailed in a series of emails[7] posted at NUblog, a representative from Apple turned down his request.

When Clark posted the email correspondence on his site, Harry Pforzheimer, Edelman's Western region president, sent him a cease-and-desist email,[8] which Clark also posted.

In the email, dated May 1, Pforzheimer wrote, "I find your tone and actions completely unjustifiable, malicious, slanderous, unprofessional and creating an extremely serious legal issue for yourself. Further, your request for an interview was not on behalf of a credentialed publication and therefore, you have no claim or right to or for a formal interview."

Clark's reaction? Let's talk credentials.

On his year-old weblog, the Toronto-based blogger has written nearly 150 tech-themed articles. Some are rants, in the grand tradition of online self-publishing, but others are thoughtful expositions on a wide range of topics, including Napster, digital cinema and online content. Clark is also working on a book about Web accessibility, and while he no longer writes freelance articles for newspaper or magazines ("I refuse to sign the contracts"), he has 390 published articles to his credit, in venues ranging from *Technology Review* to *Entertainment Weekly*.

"I may not be Ted Koppel but that doesn't mean I don't have credibility on the specific topic I'm writing about," he says.

Then again, Clark intended to write about OS X's localization features on NUblog, where a typical article garners 300 to 900 page views, according to his log files. (His stories about the Edelman incident drew several times more readers, thanks to key links on other blogs.)

Clark's request was one of several hundred that Edelman received that week, according to Pforzheimer. "Certainly, PR people have to understand weblogs as a new media outlet, but there have to be some guidelines as to who is valid and invalid as a member of the media," Pforzheimer says. "If you're calling up and saying you're a member of the media, and you're going to post something, that's one thing, but if you're somebody else who just has a site and you want to rant about something, you're not a journalist."

Edelman has accommodated interview requests from webloggers and online journalists in the past, Pforzheimer says. But, he admits, since it's hard to know whom to trust in the Wild West of weblogging, he tends to help out bloggers who are affiliated with legitimate news organizations in their day jobs, for example, Dan Gillmor, a reporter for the *San Jose Mercury News*.

"This way, I know that what they're writing about is something they've researched, that they have an opinion. It gives an added degree of comfort," Pforzheimer says.

To Clark, it's not the size of his audience that should matter, but the quality. NUblog caters to a core group of programmers, designers, and other tech-heads, who crave coverage of esoteric topics like the multi-language capabilities of a new computer platform.

"If I were trying to get an interview with Steve Jobs, who am I kidding? But since this is a small effort to fulfill my request, I can't see any reason why they couldn't do it," he says, adding: "In the post-*Ain't-It-Cool-News* era, I thought it was clear that small sites can either have a large readership or just the right readership."

What PR companies need to learn, Clark says, "is that the Internet is not a mass medium. It's all about niches, so if you have a mainstream product or service and you need to market it intelligently, then you should court these niche sources."

Swerling of Annenberg says that these niches are one of the Internet's primary strengths. "You can segment your audiences and really target your groups, and communicate with narrow groups a lot more effectively." The problem, he notes, is figuring out how thinly to slice the audience segment. "If it gets down to microniching, where do you draw the line? You can only deal with so many requests at a time."

Regardless, Clark thinks that applications for media access should be judged on their own merits, and not according to some standard of journalistic hierarchy that places blogs in the "delete message" heap. In this case, "the entire exchange probably cost Apple more than if they had just fulfilled my request," he says.

Maybe so, but Pforzheimer says the outcome of Edelman's squabble with Clark was worthwhile because it triggered a deeper discussion at the company about journalistic credentials. "We have learned a lot more about webloggers than we did before," Pforzheimer says. Who, then, is a valid journalist? "We still don't know. The dialogue continues."

Let Slip the Blogs of War

Tim Cavanaugh
January 17, 2002

GERALDO HAD TO GO ALL THE WAY TO AFGHANISTAN TO GET LOST[1] IN the "fog of war," and look how much that little episode cost all of us. If the self-hating self-promoter had really wanted to learn about confusion, at a more reasonable cost, he could have just stayed home and read the war blogs.

For it is in spending time with the war blogs that one comes to know the chaos, the inhumanity, the ultimate futility of war.

You can try to keep all the blog news straight in your head, to render a chronicle fit for posterity, but the fog of war blogging will get you. Where did I read that pithy comment about Arab paranoia 23 minutes ago? Was it by Virginia Postrel[2] or Andrew Sullivan,[3] or was it one of those other guys[4] who's always saying how great Virginia Postrel and Andrew Sullivan are? Or no, wait, maybe it was the blog by the guy who thinks Mickey Kaus[5] and Sullivan are geniuses and always links to their blogs, but thinks Postrel is an idiot—and always links to her blog to prove it?

Am I reading the article in praise of blogs[6] or the one about how bloggers have got the mainstream media on the run?[7] Hey, wait! Both of these articles remind me of that article I saw on somebody's blog about how the bloggers are revolutionizing the very way we think of news. Who did that one? Was it Glenn Reynolds?[8] Nick Denton?[9] Did Ken Layne[10] give a shout-out to something Matt Welch[11] had on his blog, and did Welch give a back-atcha link to Layne's blog? Or was it the other way around?

And shoot, where did I see that awesome takedown of Barbara Kingsolver's latest stupid column? Was that one at Buzzmachine-dot-com?[12] At Bearstrong-dot-net?[13] Blogorama-dot-com?[14] Blogsofwar-dot-blogspot?[15] Littlegreenfootballs-dot-com?[16] Moonfarmer-dot-org[17]? Warblogger-dot-blog?

A few hours of this kind of action and even the toughest war blogger is ready for a VA nuthouse.

The weblog is not the most useless weapon in the War On Terrorism. That title is still held by the nuclear submarine. But it is precisely their unconventional methods that make the war bloggers enemies to be feared. Like al-Qaeda, the war bloggers are a loosely structured network, a shadowy underground whose flexibility and compulsive log-rolling make them as cost-effective as they are deadly. Kill Glenn Reynolds and a thousand James Tarantos will rise in his place. Try to apply the Powell Doctrine and the war bloggers will elude our grasp. Ignore them and they'll use our own weapons against us.

Whence came the war blogs? You'd need a new A. J. P. Taylor[18] to answer that one. If there's one thing bloggers enjoy almost as much as fluffing each others' efforts, it's arguing over who created blogging.

The blogging community was recently torn by controversy when Joanne Jacobs[19] failed to show sufficient knowledge of blog history. (Jacobs's experience in the field began in 2001, the great era of celeblogs that allowed professional writers like Sullivan, Kaus and Joshua Micah Marshall to post their writings online, at prices more accurately reflecting their value.)

Old-timey bloggers hit Jacobs with newbie wedgies,[20] and, for people who have never seen Doug Block's Home Page,[21] there was even an appeal to Rebecca Blood's history[22] of blogging.

You might imagine weblogs were never really invented, instead evolving from earlier species dating back to Suck,[23] Justin Hall,[24] NetSurf[25] and beyond; but in our hearts, we'll always find Creationism more appealing than Darwinism.

But the appearance of the war blogs makes for a quantum leap in the history of blogging. As President Eisenhower said,[26] "This conjunction of an immense military establishment and a large arms industry is new in the American experience."

The War On Terrorism, with all its world-historical moment, has combined with the relentless drive of the bloggers to create an explosion of unfathomed energy, vitality, and pure wind. Everybody's a winner.

Glenn Reynolds[27]—whose title "Instapundit" merrily undermines his credibility (or at least foregrounds his lack of credibility)—doesn't have to be content with zinging Cornel West when he can rail against the treachery of the Saudis. Postrel[28] gets to take on serious issues of rights and security where otherwise she might just be noting how some taxicab eureka[29] she had proves the necessity of privatizing Social Security. *Best of the Web* editor James Taranto, who in some alternative universe has nothing else to discuss except how the Democrats are shamelessly using Enron as payback for Whitewater, now gets to pre-empt every argument with what appears to be the only weapon in his argumentative arsenal: "Don't you know there's a war on?"[30]

More intriguingly, the rise of war blogs has made room for a host of new players.

The Muslim Pundit[31] is "[g]oing after starry pan-Islamic futurists with a rubber glove and a sharp stick." Dr. Frank[32] gets to lambaste *The Times* for publishing what he considers a sympathetic portrait of dead Palestinian Raed al-Karmi. (Well, actually, he sort of links to Charles Johnson's blog,[33] which does the lambasting.)

Perhaps the most encouraging is Bjørn Stærk's Bearstrong.net.[34] Stærk appears to be a young Norwegian, and his command of the English idiom alone is impressive; but he's also staked out a refreshing spot as a European with generally pro-American views, and puts forth some cogent comments. An oddly touching recent post contained an unfavorable close reading of a request to be excused from military service Stærk himself sent to the Norwegian government four years ago. (In one of those "He saved my ass during the Tet Offensive" reminiscences common to war bloggers, Stærk also contends that if it weren't for erstwhile fulltime blogger Ken Layne, "I wouldn't even be blogging . . . ").

To date, Stærk's only lapse has been in failing to blog the gay marriage[35] of Per-Kristian Foss, Norway's Conservative finance minister—that story had to be picked up by Mark Morford, the *San Francisco Chronicle's* in-house blogger.[36]

These DIY self-publishers may not be treated to vomit-inducing elegies[37] by the likes of Ron Rosenbaum, but they're now solidly in the weblog loop with Sullivan and the other bigshots.

And there are plenty more where they came from, millions of bloggers ready to do their part for the struggle. Some may see America's bounty in its immeasurable fields of grain, its implacable martial power, or its 20 brands of douches. I prefer to see the triumph of the West in its numberless bloggers.

Surely when he has a chance to check out the Web, bin Laden must get a worrisome hint of Ernie Pyle's survey of the jetsam on Omaha Beach: "Behind us were such enormous replacements for this wreckage on the beach that you could hardly conceive of the sum total. Men and equipment were flowing from England in such a gigantic stream that it made the waste on the beachhead seem like nothing at all, really nothing at all."

As this may indicate, the war bloggers are a hawkish bunch. Sure, Gabrielle Taylor's Moonfarmer[38] presents a fairly catholic link collection with little commentary. Brian Lamb calls his Blowback[39] a "link-bearer for alienated left-wing bloggers everywhere," and he's got the links to *The Guardian* to prove it.

But for the most part the war bloggers are toughened desktop Guderians committed to the belief that the terrorists will win if our blogs fall silent.

"*This*, my friends, is what pisses me off about the far left," fumes[40] Damian Penny. "By the way, ignore those upcoming explosions in the Bekaa Valley," *soi-disant* Christian Christopher Johnson hisses[41] at tiny Lebanon. "In a matter of months, we have rid one major country, Afghanistan, of its Islamo-fascist tyrants and profoundly shifted another, Pakistan," great Sullivan gloats. Even the wholly unmartial Jeff Jarvis[42] gets to act like a hardass at his blog.

Of course, all these trigger-happy wits wouldn't make an effective force if they couldn't stick together. This is where mutual appreciation is critical. The tradition of blogrolling goes back a long way, but the war bloggers have made it an art form. Outside Jerry Lewis telethons, I can't remember the last time I've seen so many references to "my good friend so-and-so," "consistently excellent work by X," and so on. (Sullivan, for whom countless commentators are friends of the "dear," "good," or "old" varieties, is a particularly awful example.) A brief list of actual citations from recent war blogs:

" . . . the consistently correct Moira Breen."

"Mark Steyn—this guy is so good!"

"Dan Kennedy has an excellent piece . . . "

". . . Natalija Radic really hit them where it hurts."

"Another terrific Matt Welch column."

"Leave it to Natalie Solent to come up with something of substance."

"Professor Reynolds, once again, puts it best."

"More great comments on 'post-political correctness' from Jeff Jarvis:"

"JASON SOON has an interesting piece on . . . "

"I recommend Henry Porter's thoughtful analysis of how and why Britain's doves got just about everything wrong . . . "

"GERALDO IS A LIAR, according to a persuasive post by Joanne Jacobs."

"It's all great, but here's my favorite passage:"

"I JUST RAN ACROSS THIS COOL COLUMN BY MATT WELCH."

"MOIRA BREEN DEMOLISHES FEMINIST WHINING"

"A very good post from Thomas Nephew on Tom "Do Nothing" Ridge."

"JOSH MARSHALL has an interesting point about Enron."

"Well what do you know, it looks like my friend Ed Mazza has his crafty own webpage now."

"So good to see that superposter Glenn Reynolds is human and does have a life."

"My very dear friend Ken Layne weighs in on some sort of competition over who has been doing these weblog thingies the longest."

"Instapundit is right: Today brings us a particulary good rant/bleat/sermon from James Lileks. He has the guts to say that, yes, Western culture is superior."

"I don't know who 'Dr. Frank' is, beyond seemingly being a yank living in the U.K., but he runs a terrific blog that you should check out. He also says nice things about me, which is pleasant. "

"I've been meaning to thank another weblog, the Little Green Footballs, which sends a bit of traffic to this site."

And if all those kind words aren't enough, the war bloggers never leave a man behind. Each blogger's page contains—along with a forlorn Tipjar[43] pitch—a comprehensive list of links to other bloggers. (Speaking of which: If I haven't mentioned your blog, I apologize, but I guarantee some link in this article has your blog within one degree of separation.) "Absolutely everyone has linked to this, and no wonder," Natalie Solent swoons[44] over a choice bit by some fellow blogger.

The second element of war blogging—and perhaps the one that makes it distinctive—is the frequent deployment of straw men. If the bloggers are fighting a world war, Barbara Kingsolver is their enigma code. Without the hapless *Poisonwood Bible* author, we'd never be quite sure who we're fighting. Layne[45] and Welch[46] have both used her for target practice. Other bloggers remember her like the *Maine* (and Kingsolver does them all the favor of clearly having no idea what she's talking about[47]).

But make no mistake: our washrooms are breeding pacifists, and the war bloggers know who they are: Ted Rall. Susan Sontag. Arundhati Roy. Barbara Ehrenreich. Noam Chomsky. Ralph Nader. The names of shame, the Quislings and public enemies of the blog lands, they are shown no mercy. When Stephanie Salter—one of those professional Catholics[48] who tend to write big-city columns—worked up an ill-considered Jesus piece[49] for the *Chronicle*, the bloggers let her have it.

Christopher Johnson[50] laid down suppressing fire. James Lileks[51] called in air strikes. The fortunately named Steven DenBeste[52] made a flanking action. The dour Joanne Jacobs[53] got her in the crossfire.

And Glenn Reynolds[54] himself came in for the kill. It was an inevitable outcome: if there's one thing the war bloggers hate more than the newspapers from which they cop all their stories, it's the OpEd writers who work for those papers.

Which brings us to the third leg of war blogging: agitation. The bloggers boldly declare that they are in favor of our war on terrorism—a courageous stand when only 107 percent of the population supports the war effort, but one that's hard to keep up when all the bloggers are in agreement. This can lead to some pretty thin outrages and crabbed arguments. When Taranto seethes that the Spanish have no right to quibble about our death penalty because, well, because Spain was a fascist dictatorship as recently as 1975, you know you've reached some kind of low point in the art of forensic rhetoric.

Worse, this situation makes the entire blog universe resemble nothing so much as a giant listserv populated exclusively by dittoheads. How many different ways are there to be scandalized by the WTC monument[55] hubbub? So the trick is not just to signal your agreement with some fellow blogger, but to really *exclaim* your agreement, possibly with repetitions and even multiple exclamation points. Search a while and you'll find many examples like Charles Murtaugh's[56] rave for "Jonah Goldberg's great, and I mean damn great column about the relationship between technology and liberty."

Do the war bloggers have an Achilles' heel? They do.

For all the bitching they log about the mainstream media, none of the bloggers are actually cruising the streets of Peshawar or Aden or Mogadishu. Thus, they're wholly dependent upon that very same mainstream media. You can cut on *Salon* all you like, Mr. Blogger, but they have a man in Afghanistan. Do you?

There's a pretty severe disconnect here, between some of the most bouyant down-with-the-media-elite skylarking we've seen since 1995-era Jon Katz, and the fact that those same media elites are providing virtually all of the news the war bloggers congratulate themselves on serving up. And serving it up none too quickly. Australian blogger Tim Blair[57] has a distinct advantage in that Australians use some futuristic time anomaly to see 18 hours into the future.

But for consistently being first to find links to growing stories, Matt Drudge (whose relationship to mainstream reporting is infinitely more complex than the bloggers') is still far ahead of the pack, and the result is that after taking in the *Drudge Report*, you frequently spend the next 36 hours being alerted to the existence of some breaking story that you've already read.

These are real structural challenges for the war bloggers. Will they pull it through, and live up to the hype? After all their tough-guy posturing, will they be hard enough to crush their enemies? At war's end, will they return, like veterans of so many wars, bitter and disillusioned and jobless?

I say nay! For the battle-hardened war bloggers, the future is almost as bright as the present. I can almost picture the happy few knocking back drinks at the blogger officers' club:

"Man, if I didn't have this blog to do I'd be over there in Tora Bora right now!"

"Yeah, what can you do? War's a young man's game. They also serve who stand and wait. I think the American people have realized how important the war blogs are to our security."

"Well it ain't easy. I had some tough blogging today. Blogspot intelligence told me not to expect the punditry to be heavy, but we ran into a battalion-strength pacifist column with Sontag support, and we were low on rants. For a while I didn't think I was gonna make it, but around 1800 hours I laid down a barrage of trenchant observations and we finally broke through."

"Hell, those pampered OpEd columnists will never know what it's like at the front. Out here you either blog your way out or you get dead!"

"Wow, that's a keen observation. Let me go link to that in my blog."

Shine on, you crazy bloggers! Someday the rest of us will hold our manhoods cheap that we did not blog with you this day. But as long as courage lives and liberty endures, every American will be proud to have you out there, blogging for an audience of none.

PART SIX

Community

33

Building an Online Community: Just Add Water

Matt Haughey
August 18, 2001

I'M FREQUENTLY ASKED HOW METAFILTER[1] CAME TO BE, WHAT the secret is, and what I've learned in the process of building it. I didn't have a tidy plan or set path when I started. I watched several big communities grow from nothing and prosper and I took my lead from them, but a good lot of what I know now was gained from trial and error. During those first few months, I picked up a lot of experience in dealing with new members, and got a chance to try out several different techniques to help growth and deal with problems. I noticed a lot of trends, I made a few mistakes, but above all I learned a lot in the process.

I'm here today to tell you the dos-and-don'ts of building a website community, but I can only give general guidelines. Every community is different, and every administrator of a community is different, so an aspiring community leader needs to adjust accordingly.

. . . In case you were wondering, the title is a bit of a joke, building a website into a vibrant community filled with many contributors is very difficult and it is impossible to break down the exact steps, but I'll do my best.

1. Make Sure You Really Want to Do This

You know how interviewers ask someone who has lived a full life and is near death, if they could relive their life again, what they would do different. You have to ask yourself that before you lift a finger building a community. Are you ready to be a leader? Are you ready to do all the work necessary to create not just a normal, engaging website, but one that many others can use? Are you ready to spend every waking moment watching it? Are you ready to stay up all night re-coding main areas of the site after someone hacks the files? Are you ready to keep it up, day in and day out for as long as you can stand it?

I can't underestimate how much time you will spend on a community website. It will take longer to create, often months to get rolling, with constant tweaking and twiddling of the code to keep everything running smoothly. I was lucky when I started MetaFilter because at that point in my life, I had plenty of free time, I was itching to learn a new programming language, and I had a laid-back job where I could take lots of little breaks to check in on the site. If someone asked me if I'd do it all over again starting today with my current life, I probably wouldn't, because I don't really have the time and energy to start a new multi-user community site from scratch.

This is the most challenging point in the list, but it's good to get this one figured out before you plunge full speed into new development.

2. Have Both a Compelling Idea and Compelling Content

There are lots of possible reasons to start a community, but generally it's good to focus on a specific topic. Having a specific topic means you'll have an easier time explaining your site's purpose, and quickly find like-minded people to contribute their thoughts and content to your community. MetaFilter was created with the loosest of intentions, to simply have a weblog that covered anything on the Web, and it took about nine months of daily posting before anyone noticed it existed. I guess having comments and allowing others to post was a compelling enough idea that led to a busy site, but a frequent question from first time visitors was (and still is) "What's this site all about?" If my site was a model airplane owner's group site with a well-defined mission and idea for its purpose, I'm sure I could have found other members a lot sooner.

Compelling content is more important than you probably think. The most well-defined group purpose, with lots of motivated members, will go nowhere unless there is something to draw everyone together and get people contributing. This rule could go for any site really, but it's important to have the best possible writing, design, photography, etc. that you can, and update as often as possible. This is where community sites can excel over single person operations. With a diverse enough membership, you can have an expert artist, fantastic writers, great photographers, and senior programmers to build the best community site imaginable, and everyone pitching in can update the content on a frequent basis. It's not exactly easy to get big membership numbers on which to draw for ongoing content; first you have to convince people to join your site, and contribute or comment on other work, and for that you need to start with good content. It's sort of a catch–22, but once you get a group of members creating good content, it creates a strong positive feedback loop that leads to growth, popularity, and quality.

3. Seed Content Sets the Stage

In the early months of a community site, it's important that there is good content there, and that the comments or audience interaction are as close to optimal as possible, so that others reading the site can get a feel for how they are expected to act. If you're building a site that covers politics and you're dreaming of lively debate with a specific slant, make sure your first few articles, essays, or threads cover a good topic, and that some discussion follows where users (more than one) are debating things in an intelligent way. New members will see what is currently on the site, and react accordingly. If there is considerate and helpful criticism, others will usually follow. If there are "first posts!" and posts making threats on other members, other such garbage will follow that as well.

If it's a company discussion forum, set up some threads and have some friends start discussions. If it's a community of airplane enthusiasts, try and find two or three people to help start the site off the same way, by finding content and discussing it in a proper manner. You're not shooting for having hundreds of fake discussion posts with no one; you're just trying to convey a code of conduct by starting with things you can use as examples, and new members can follow.

4. Create Some Basic Guidelines and Be As Fair As Possible

When you're the administrator on a community site, it's important that you set the examples to follow. Post regularly and intelligently, and keep a high profile on the site so others know of your presence (this keeps some troublemakers away, since they know that the site owner will quickly catch wind of their mischief). Follow the Golden Rule,[2] treat others as you would like to be treated, and watch for unsavory patterns that form. If you catch something that's happening with some regularity, and you'd like to see it stop, make it part of the rules of the site, and explain somewhere why people shouldn't do it (start by putting a pointer somewhere near the posting forms, so curious contributors can read them if they like). Keep track of these rules, and put them somewhere people can easily find them on the site. When you have to enforce them, be nice about it, and show people the rules and how they broke them. The world isn't a black-and-white place, so a lot of things will be up to your judgement, but explain as fully as you can why you chose to enforce a certain thing, and point out what the person can do to prevent it from happening again.

What users of a community don't want to see is a headstrong leader who rules with an iron fist, and seems to take pleasure in enforcement. Users also don't want to see a leader that changes his or her mind from day to day, enforcing rules with some users, while letting friends or long time members get away with murder. Users don't want to be yelled at publicly when they make their first mistake, and they want to be given second chances. Fairness and consistency are key practices when you're running an online community.

5. Have a Place to Talk About the Site, Somewhere on the Site

I've had a lot of success with a special section of MetaFilter designed to talk about issues around the site, bugs and features users wish for, or any etiquette that may have been breached, and I created it because I noticed people were talking about the site on the site itself fairly regularly. Gone unchecked, I noticed it created circular discussions where people talked about other parts of the site on the site itself and it appeared to be senseless navelgazing. Having a separate section conveniently allows that to run in an organized fashion, while at the same time keeping the main site free of looking like one big game of Duck-Duck-Goose. It doesn't necessarily have to be on the site itself, or even on the web. It could be a many-to-many email list for interested parties to participate in, if that will easier for you to implement.

6. Spread the Work Out As Much As Possible

If it's possible, have a few trusted friends act as moderators and administrators and allow people to contribute and streamline the code that runs the site. When the day-to-day maintenance can be spread out among several people, it's okay if someone goes on vacation, gets busy with work or gets ill, or takes some time off from the site. If lots of new features are being requested, several people can work on them, and debug them faster. This situation isn't always possible, and there are only a few projects that come to mind, such as evolt.org[3] where a sizeable, diverse group keeps a site running.

7. Deal with Troublemakers As Quickly and Nicely As Possible

If you're running a community site of some sort, there's a good chance that people are going to try and mess with it, push the envelope, and hack at it for no good reason. The important thing for you to do as the administrator is deal with problem members as soon as possible and as carefully as possible. If you act rashly or too strongly, you may incite a casual hacker into a full-blown making-your-life-a-living-hell type of hacker. You want to defuse any situation before it gets out of hand.

Start by emailing the person as soon as you can (but give yourself a little time to think; don't send anything too rashly or in the heat of the moment) and asking them gently if perhaps they didn't catch the guidelines pages, or that you'd prefer if they did their thing in a different way. Be careful of your wording in these emails—you don't want to sound threatening or patronizing in any way. You might want to have a friend review the message before sending it to make sure it's neither of those things. A short email reminding a trouble-making member of the error of their ways can usually take care of 90% of problems. Even if a member is doing something obviously malicious, they'll usually stop when called on it.

If that doesn't stop the problem member, the next thing to do is enforce some sort of penalty. This would usually be something like taking away posting rights or moderation rights, posing some new limit on their participation in the site. You will probably want to email them, letting them know what you've done, why you've done it, and most importantly what they can do to get the ban lifted. Hopefully, you'll never need to proceed after these first two measures because a situation can quickly escalate into a war of willpower. If you have to start banning members, doing so will prove quite difficult. You may take all rights away from their account, block their IP address or range of IP addresses, and/or remove their contributions from the site. There are trickier means of hiding a problem user's activity from the rest, but I won't go into that here. It's not a path you'll ever want to take, and no one "wins" in the end; it's just a big waste of energy for all involved.

The bottom line is to stop unsavory behavior by defusing nasty situations as early as possible, in as nice of a way as possible.

8. Highlight the Good, Recognize the Work of Others

I'm still searching for the perfect way to do this, but you'll encourage good contributions by recognizing and highlighting the best your community has to offer. This is especially true when your community is larger, and you need something to point to as a casual "Hall of Fame" that new users can take their cue from. This can take many forms: you can use voting/moderation to let the community pick its favorites, you can utilize some sort of Brownie Point system where members earn credits for good contributions which are displayed somewhere (an ego stroking stop, basically), or if you're lacking the extra technology, just keep track of them by hand in a "Best of" setting.

Building an inviting place that attracts users and maintaining high quality content on a bustling community site is far from easy, but these key points should help get you going in the right direction.

34

Good Links vs. Good Discussion: A MetaFilter Discussion

MetaFilter.com
January 14, 2002

Good links vs. good discussion: Which is more important? And why is it so difficult to find both in an FPP lately?
posted by dogmatic to metafilter-related at 8:19 AM PST

Because the best links are to things which are beautiful or thought-provoking or informative and Web-based, the best discussions often seem to spring from poll-type situations or arguments about current events. Sadly, when posts which are meant to trigger good discussions don't, you're usually not left with anything really worthwhile.
posted by snarkout at 8:28 AM PST on January 14

There's been a lot of bitching about what's more important—the link or the subsequent discussion. Right now it seems that MeFi is divided into two camps: one that comes here for interesting links and one that comes here for interesting discussion. Generally, it seems that the older users appreciate links while newer users skew toward discussion. Is there a way to bridge this rift? If not, what's the future of MeFi?
posted by dogmatic at 8:39 AM PST on January 14

Speaking personally I like both, if there's some sort of equilibrium.

The key words for me when thinking about FPPs are *unique things [. . .] find on the web* (from the about page) and *most people haven't seen [. . .] before* (from the guidelines). I believe (stop me if I'm wrong, I wasn't here) that the original purpose of metafilter was to spark discussion about unique or original content on the Web. The problem, if there is one, is that there seems to be a lot of discussion lately about things that just aren't unique, such as news links to CNN et al.

There's also the point of view that this is a community and anything a community does is, de facto, its purpose. It's probably a hard thing to bear if you join a community for one purpose and then that purpose appears to change under your nose.

posted by walrus at 8:58 AM PST on January 14

As an 'older user,' I do come for links, but I also look forward to discussions on those links. I think the perception that 'older users' prefer links to discussion is that there have been complaints about so much news-centric links and most discussions occurring around those items rather than other types of discussions (non-politics, non-religion, non-Dubya, etc.).

There seems more of a competition to post the first occurrence of a news item rather than something interesting from the Web.

As for the lack of variety—I blame that on the previous[1] reasons mentioned—mainly the lack of new blood / more heterogenous participation.

posted by rich at 9:13 AM PST on January 14

Some people confuse 'good discussion' with 'a long page of comments.'

Long pages of comments are frequently not discussions; they're either a list of subjective opinions (resulting from poll posts) or arguments (resulting from troll posts).

I don't think the emphasis should be on good *discussion*. There might be a good FPP with only a few comments after it, but the *reading* (or listening) is the worthwhile part.

In the case of the recent FPPs talking about bands, there are long pages of listed subjective opinions. People might like them because (a) they can reply to the post because it's highly likely that they have some opinion about some band, and (b) they can have their opinions affirmed by others' posts: "I like that band too!"—but that doesn't mean that it's a very worthwhile 'discussion,' or that it's even a discussion at all.

posted by kv at 9:18 AM PST on January 14

I think we have to admit that we're not going to solve the world's problems here; we're unlikely to convince anyone that their long-held opinions are invalid; we're unlikely to get trolls to stop trolling or idiots to stop, um, idioting. The best we can do is (a) not shit on Matt's work, (b) ignore blatant trolling and id-iocy, (c) play nice, and (d) be the best poster/commenter you can be. The more people that can do that, the better MetaFilter will be for everyone.

posted by UncleFes at 9:33 AM PST on January 14

I chatted with Matt very briefly about this sort of thing after the Cleveland Browns bottle-throwing thread I posted a few weeks ago. It seems there is a Zen koan for MetaFilter:

Current events and other discussions that were not originally meant to be on MetaFilter are becoming the acceptable norm, but they're also contributing to the eventual demise of MetaFilter.

I had a long essay written here using the "worst band of all time" thread as an example, but I don't think it belongs here. Let's just say, really think about what you're posting and try to pro-mote good, thoughtful discussion.

posted by starvingartist at 9:51 AM PST on January 14

I hate sports analogies and I hate baseball, but here goes: posting is like pitching, the batter is the first comment, the ensuing commenting is the infield and outfield, mefi cops are first, third and home base umpires, all the fans in the stadium are lurkers, and Matt's the Comish. Everyone is necessary, and it's beautiful to watch and play. . . . oh well, I gave it a try.
   posted by Voyageman at 10:10 AM PST on January 14

. . . and the hot dog salesman is from Portugal.
   Yeah, it all makes sense.
   posted by mathowie at 10:19 AM PST on January 14

perritos calientes
   posted by Voyageman at 10:25 AM PST on January 14

Does that make clavdivs the "SOY BOMB" guy?
   posted by Marquis at 10:52 AM PST on January 14

I think waxpancake's post[2] today is in the vein of classic MetaFilter, an amazing find you wouldn't normally see unless thousands of pairs of eyes were scouring the Web for interesting bits.
   There's not much to discuss about the links, but it's a great post.
   posted by mathowie at 11:03 AM PST on January 14

perritos calientes
   That would be *cachorros quentes* in Portuguese, Voyageman. [*lower lip starts strembling*] I may be your hot dog salesman [*tears begin streaming*] . . . but . . . but I have my pride!
   posted by MiguelCardoso at 11:03 AM PST on January 14

Clavdivs is the guy who whispers crazytalk into Jaron Lanier's ears while he preps his dreads.
   posted by UncleFes at 2:00 PM PST on January 14

Right now it seems that MeFi is divided into two camps: one that comes here for interesting links and one that comes here for interesting discussion.

I would argue this point. This business of 'two camps' may sound good, but I don't think it's true—or, rather, I think it's an oversimplification.

It's 'Fork! Spoon!' once again—i.e., an argument that is merely vociferous agreement. We all know the history and I'm not going to belabour the point—I would simply suggest that most people enjoy both good FPPs *and* good discussion, to various degrees, and at various times.

It may not all be good, but it's fruitless to identify 'division into camps' where none exists, as those polarized camps will spring up at the very suggestion they do exist.

posted by stavrosthewonderchicken at 4:44 PM PST on January 14

. . . and the hot dog salesman is from Portugal.

. . . and the beer vendor is from Bridgeport, Connecticut.

Sorry, had to stake my claim.

posted by jonmc at 7:03 PM PST on January 14

Or, what about a self-rating system on each FPP like what's done at evolt.org?

That sounds pretty interesting, but I wonder how many people will vote along political lines. I doubt a pro-Bush post would reach the top here. I'm also curious to know if people will vote strictly on the FPP or consider the discussion too. A great post could turn into a trollish exchange very quickly; it doesn't seem fair that a great post should be knocked to the bottom of the page because so-and-so can't stop using the phrase "Emperor Asscroft."

I'm not saying it's a bad idea, I'd love to see it implemented just to see how it eventually pans out. I'm sure it's a lot of work but if

Matt is considering adding moderation to comments, he could use a lot of the same code to do FPPs too.
> posted by skallas at 7:15 PM PST on January 14

Spoon!
> posted by stavrosthewonderchicken at 8:20 PM PST on January 14

The anti-Spoon thread is next door.[3] This is being-hit-on-the-head lessons in here.
> posted by stavrosthewonderchicken at 9:24 PM PST on January 14

spoon?[4]
> posted by walrus at 1:15 AM PST on January 15

Um, guys? There is no Spoon.
> posted by j.edwards at 1:30 AM PST on January 15

People, people, there's a simple hardware solution to this problem: The Spork[5]
> posted by dchase at 6:10 AM PST on January 15

SPORK!
I don't think a thread rating would really work. It would get caught in the momentum just as posting does . . . and I see people abusing it more than it being useful.
> posted by rich at 6:11 AM PST on January 15

Spoon[6] any day.
> posted by Voyageman at 10:56 AM PST on January 15

Notes

Chapter 1

1. http://www.camworld.com/
2. http://slashdot.org/features/99/05/13/1832251.shtml
3. http://www.robotwisdom.com/
4. http://www.theobvious.com/archives/112299.html
5. http://www.thelegacyproject.net/
6. http://www.soulflare.com/
7. http://www.0sil8.com/
8. http://www.sfstories.com/index.shtml?19
9. http://www.powazek.com/nikon/ispunaroundwithit.html, http://www.powazek.com/nikon/iputitinmymouth.html, http://www.powazek.com/nikon/iranbyitlikealunatic.html
10. http://www.wrongwaygoback.com/
11. http://www.wrongwaygoback.com/wjh/jocks.shtml
12. http://scriptingnews.userland.com/backIssues/2000/02/16
13. http://www.megnut.com/
14. http://www.saturn.org/
15. http://www.saturn.org/
16. http://www.blogger.com/

Chapter 2

1. http://www.robotwisdom.com
2. http://www.jjg.net/infosift/
3. http://www.camworld.com/
4. http://www.jjg.net/portal/tpoowl.html
5. http://www.peterme.com
6. http://www.eatonweb.com/
7. http://portal.eatonweb.com/
8. http://www.pitas.com
9. http://www.pyra.com
10. http://www.groksoup.com
11. http://www.editthispage.com
12. http://www.cockybastard.com/
13. http://www.useit.com/alertbox/980906.html
14. http://deoxy.org/seize_it.htm
15. http://www.evhead.com/
16. http://www.megnut.com/

17. http://www.metafilter.com
18. http://www.weblogs.com/
19. http://www.eatonweb.com/portal/portal.php3
20. http://www.blogger.com/directory/lastUpdateDirectory_1.pyra

Chapter 3

1. http://camworld.com/
2. http://www.camworld.com/journal/rants/99/01/26.html
3. http://www.smug.com/
4. http://www.flutterby.com/
5. http://www.scripting.com/
6. http://www.robotwisdom.com/
7. http://www.theobvious.com/
8. http://www.obscurestore.com/
9. http://www.memepool.com/
10. http://www.csmonitor.com/durable/1999/05/12/fp6s2-csm.shtml
11. http://www.jjg.net/
12. http://peterme.com/

Chapter 4

1. http://www.manifestation.com/
2. http://www.camworld.com/list/
3. http://www.mcs.net/~jorn/html/weblogs/weblog.html
4. http://www.memepool.com/
5. http://www.jjg.net/
6. http://www.flutterby.com/
7. http://www.theobvious.com/
8. http://www.scripting.com/
9. http://htp.felter.org/
10. http://www.userland.com/
11. http://www.obscurestore.com/

Chapter 5

1. http://www.robotwisdom.com/
2. http://tr.pair.com/
3. http://www.cardhouse.com/links/weblog.htm
4. http://www.flutterby.com/
5. http://www.obscurestore.com/
6. http://www.fcc.gov/Daily_Releases/Daily_Digest/1999/welcome.html
7. http://www.miningco.com/

Chapter 6

1. http://bradlands.com/
2. http://www.aol.com/
3. http://www.olin.wustl.edu/~bogart/
4. http://nowthis.com/log/
5. http://schroeder.wustl.edu/mach1/
6. http://www.robotwisdom.com/
7. http://www.chaparraltree.com/honeyguide/

8. http://frontier.userland.com/
9. http://www.scripting.com/
10. http://www.camworld.com/
11. http://www.peterme.com/
12. http://tr.pair.com/
13. http://www.whump.com/moreLikeThis/index.php3
14. http://bradlands.com/
15. http://www.windowseat.org/weblog/
16. http://directory.mozilla.org/Computers/Internet/WWW/Best_of_the_Web/
Personal/Web_Logs/
17. http://www.camworld.com/journal/rants/99/01/26.html
18. http://www.camworld.com/list/
19. http://www.windowseat.org/weblog/
20. http://www.camworld.com/
21. http://www.robotwisdom.com/

Chapter 7

1. http://www.zeldman.com/coming.html, http://www.scripting.com/,
http://www.onfocus.com/, http://www.mempool.com/,
http://accidental.plastiqueweb.com/index2.html, http://www.oneswellfoop.com/wwww/,
http://www.pocketgeek.com/pith/, http://www.bluishorange.com/,
http://www.robotwisdom.com/, http://www.windowseat.org/weblog/,
http://www.tvpicks.net/, http://www.metafilter.com/, http://www.yupislyr.com/weblog/,
http://www.gooddeed.net/blog/, http://www.slightlynorth.com/,
http://www.50cups.com/strange/, http://www.wwa.com/~dhartung/weblog/,
http://www.randomfoo.net/, http://www.yoink.com/webwaste/, http://www.2xy.org/,
http://www.randomwalks.com/, http://www.flutterby.com/, http://www.calamondin.com/,
http://members.tripod.com/amused_2/weblog.html, http://gilbert.pitas.com/,
http://www.mthology.com/, http://www.davidgagne.net/, http://www.wockerjabby.com/,
http://www.littleyellowdiffernet.com/
2. http://www.riothero.com/, http://www.uncorked.org/medley/,
http://www.chrish.org/, http://www.gumbopages.com/looka/,
http://www.foreword.com/danelope.php, http://www.jish.nu/,
http://wmf.editthispage.com/, http://www.mrbarrett.com/,
http://stommel.tamu.edu/~baum/ethel/blogger.html, http://www.viama.co.uk/blog.htm,
http://home.earthlink.net/~seymourlavey/hate/donkeymon.html,
http://www.jarrahconsulting.com.au/endor/day17/, http://gammatron.weblogger.com/,
http://www.stormwerks.com/linked/, http://www.littleyellowdifferent.com/survivor/,
http://www.megnut.com/, http://www.kottke.org/, http://www.saturn.org/,
http://www.wannabegirl.org/, http://www.swallowingtacks.com/,
http://www.anthonyjhicks.com/weblog/, http://www.bluesilver.org/random/,
http://entropy.ayu-soul.com/blog.html, http://www.geegaw.com/,
http://www.eatonweb.com/, http://www.caterina.net/, http://www.evhead.com/,
http://www.glassdog.com/linkinlog2000/, http://openlog.pitas.com/,
http://www.electricbiscuit.com/
3. http://anitar.pitas.com/, http://www.thenetstar.org/blahger/main.html,
http://www.mermaniac.com/, http://www.hit-or-miss.org/, http://www.geeknik.net/,
http://www.storm.ca/~evad/blog/, http://www.impudite.com/blog/,
http://www.zymm.com/raster/,

http://www.generation.net/~passerby/montreal/montreal.htm,
http://www.periodically.com/, http://www.psionic.nu/, http://www.gooddeed.net/tos/,
http://www.karenh.org/

4. http://www.inessential.com/, http://www.bradlands.com/weblog/,
http://www.packetmonkeys.net/, http://www.misterpants.com/01/,
http://www.sixfoot6.com/, http://baylink.pitas.com/, http://www.notsosoft.com/blog/,
http://www.thinkdink.com/, http://www.larkfarm.com/weblog.asp,
http://www.peterme.com/, http://www.moronic.org/,
http://www.electrobacon.com/apathy/, http://www.mellifluous.org/,
http://techno.fissure.org/, http://www.ctrl-alt-ego.com/blog.html

5. http://www.gaylery.com/journal.html, http://swirlee.catharsis.org/,
http://www.perpetualbeta.com/weblog.html, http://www.wrongwaygoback.com/,
http://www.dansanderson.com/blog/, http://www.neoflux.com/,
http://www.stuffeddog.com/, http://www.somnolent.org/, http://www.jaut.com/jauteria/,
http://www.bryanjbusch.com/lately/, http://netdyslexia.editthispage.com/,
http://www.dansays.com/, http://www.camworld.com/, http://www.plasticbag.org/,
http://www.metagrrrl.com/, http://www.io.com/~bmokeefe/harmful/,
http://www.themaxx.com/bits/, http://q.queso.com/, http://www.rebeccablood.net/,
http://www.utsler.com/metacubed/, http://www.ntk.net/, http://www.glashier.com/blog/,
http://www.fiendishthingy.net/, http://array.editthispage.com/

6. http://www.thinkhole.org/, http://www.neilalien.com/,
http://www.dack.com/home.html, http://seniorcitizen.blogspot.com/,
http://www.genehack.org/, http://www.fasthack.com/, http://www.athens.net/~ewagoner/,
http://www.tomalak.org/, http://www.bump.net/, http://www.harrumph.com/,
http://www.backupbrain.com/, http://www.bekkoame.ne.jp/~aabb/plus9.html,
http://www.prolific.org/, http://www.sxsw.com/, http://www.cafepress.com/cujoe/,
http://www.cafepress.com/wetlog/, http://www.cafepress.com/metafilter/,
http://www.torrez.org/top/, http://www.wrongwaygoback.com/wjh/,
http://www.jish.nu/webloggers/, http://www.dansanderson.com/shf/,
http://www.utsler.com/monkeyshines/, http://www.foreword.com/blogview/,
http://www.prolific.org/archive/2000_05_07_index.shtml, http://www.blogger.com/,
http://manila.userland.com/, http://www.pitas.com/, http://www.beebo.org/metalog/ratings/,
http://www.wrongwaygoback.com/everymeeveryyou/

7. http://www.fairvue.com/
8. http://www.bradlands.com/dww/
9. http://www.linkwatcher.com/
10. http://portal.eatonweb.com/
11. http://www.larkfarm.com/growth_of_weblogs.asp

Chapter 9

1. http://www.metafilter.com/detail.cfm?link_ID=2382
2. http://www.powazek.com/2000_06_01_archive.shtml
3. http://www.samsloan.com/taylor-h.htm

Chapter 10

1. http://www.robotwisdom.com/
2. http://www.lemonyellow.com/
3. http://www.boingboing.net/
4. http://www.cardhouse.com/links/weblog.html

5. http://www.westernhomes.org/
6. http://www.peterme.com/
7. http://www.shmooze.com/yudel
8. http://www.blogger.com/

Chapter 11

1. http://www.evhead.com/
2. http://www.pyra.com/
3. http://www.blogger.com/
4. http://www.evhead.com/?archive=1999_08_01_ev.xml
5. http://www.peterme.com/
6. http://www.scripting.com/

Chapter 12

1. http://www.blogger.com/botw.pyra
2. http://www.whowouldbuythat.com/
3. http://web.0sil8.com/episodes/pressnothing/
4. http://www.tellme.com/
5. http://haiku575.blogspot.com/

Chapter 15

1. http://www.eatonweb.com/weblog/index.shtml
2. http://www.memepool.com/
3. http://www.whump.com/moreLikeThis/index.php3
4. http://www.alistapart.com/
5. http://portal.eatonweb.com/
6. http://portal.eatonweb.com/
7. http://www.camworld.com/
8. http://aaronland.net/weblog/
9. http://aaronland.net/toys/surfmenu/weblogs.html
10. http://catless.ncl.ac.uk/Lindsay/weblog/latest.html
11. http://www.azstarnet.com/~jacobs/
12. http://www.peterme.com/
13. http://www.evhead.com/
14. http://www.wwa.com/~dhartung/weblog/ (no longer functioning)
15. http://webword.com/
16. http://www.pyra.com/

Chapter 16

1. http://www.peterme.com/
2. http://www.blogger.com/
3. http://www.pitas.com/
4. http://www.manilasites.com/, http://www.weblogs.com/ or http://www.editthispage.com/
5. http://www.slashdot.org/
6. http://doc.weblogs.com/
7. http://paulandrews.manilasites.com/
8. http://weblog.mercurycenter.com/ejournal/
9. http://www.scripting.com/

10. http:// glennf.weblogs.com/
11. http://doc.weblogs.com/2001/03/27
12. http://www.google.com/
13. http://doc.weblogs.com/2001/03/28/
14. http://radio.userland.com/
15. http://www.poynter.org/medianews/

Chapter 17

1. http://www.alistapart.com/
2. http://nt.excite.com/
3. http://www.newbot.com/
4. http://www.newshub.com/
5. http://www.newslinx.com/

Chapter 20

1. http://www.geekcode.com/geek.html
2. http://resourcesforbears.com/nbcs/gennbcs.html
3. http://noahgrey.com/greysoft/
4. http://www.movabletype.org/
5. http://www.blogger.com/
6. http://www.bigblogtool.com/
7. http://www.upsaid.com/
8. http://www.blogspot.com/
9. http://www.diaryland.com/
10. http://www.livejournal.com/
11. http://www.bradlands.com/, http://www.camworld.com/,
http://www.evhead.com/, http://www.haughey.com/, http://www.kottke.org/,
http://www.megnut.com/, http://www.plasticbag.org/, http://www.powazek.com/,
http://www.rebeccablood.net/, http://www.saturn.org/, http://www.scripting.com/,
http://www.zeldman.com/

Chapter 21

1. http://www.kottke.org/
2. http://www.osil8.com/
3. http://www.zeldman.com/
4. http://www.alistapart.com/
5. http://www.harrumph.com/
6. http://www.jezebel.com/
7. http://www.blogger.com/
8. http://www.dansanderson.com/shf/
9. http://www.fairvue.com/?feature=awards2001
10. http://pine.cs.yale.edu/blogs/scoops.html
11. http://www.weblogs.com/hotList
12. http://www.torrez.org/top/

Chapter 22

1. http://tom.weblogs.com/stories/storyReader$690

Chapter 23
1. http://www.kottke.org/notes/0011.html

Chapter 26
1. http://www.lockergnome.com/manifesto-signers.html
2. http://www.wheresgeorge.com/

Chapter 27
1. Giles Turnbull

Chapter 28
1. http://www.benbrown.com/
2. http://www.benbrown.com/daily/cds.cgi?c=2000/03/21
3. http://www.oneswellfoop.com/, http://www.twernt.com/, http://www.swallowingtacks.com/
4. http://www.onfocus.com/, http://www.nullmeansnull.com/tally/, http://www.rebeccablood.net/
5. http://www.metafilter.com/
6. http://www.eatonweb.com/
7. http://www.eatonweb.com/portal/
8. http://www.diaryland.com/
9. http://www.teethmag.com/showart.pl?pid=50
10. http://www.shit.com/
11. http://www.epinions.com/
12. http://www.anyfuckingurlendingwith.nu/
13. http://www.napster.com/
14. http://www.microsoft.com/
15. http://www.wired.com/
16. http://www.zdnet.com/zdnn/stories/news/0,4586,2473689,00.html
17. http://www.saturn.org/
18. http://www.harrumph.com/
19. http://www.weblogs.com/
20. http://www.blogger.com/
21. http://myfuckingweblog.weblog.com/

Chapter 29
1. http://www.librarian.net/
2. http://ojr.usc.edu/content/story.cfm?request=330
3. http://www.content-exchange.com/weblog/weblog.htm
4. http://ojr.usc.edu/content/story.cfm/request/503/
5. http://archives.seattletimes.nwsource.com/cgi-bin/texis/web/vortex/display?slug=ptblog01&date=20010401&query=Fleishman
6. http://www.paulandrews.com/
7. http://www.webwon.com/
8. http://www.andrewsullivan.com/
9. http://www.weblogger.com/
10. http://www.blogger.com/

11. http://www.paulandrews.com/stories/storyReader$122
12. http://buzz.weblogs.com/
13. http://stacks.msnbc.com/news/535681.asp
14. http://www.monsterbuzz.com/
15. http://buzz.weblogs.com/2001/04/20
16. http://buzz.weblogs.com/2001/02/06
17. http://glennf.com/blog/
18. http://ojr.usc.edu/content/story.cfm?request=496
19. http://glennf.com/blog/2001/05/21.html
20. http://davenet.userland.com/2001/04/08/internetCriticTakesOnMicrosoft

Chapter 30

1. http://www.blogger.com/
2. http://www.weblogger.com/
3. http://www.livejournal.com/
4. http://web.siliconvalley.com/content/sv/opinion/dgillmor/weblog/
5. http://www.startribune.com/weblog
6. http://www.tvbarn.com/
7. http://www.boston.com/globe/weblog/dcdenison/
8. http://www.cq.com/scoop/
9. http://www.thescoop.org/
10. http://www.thecyberscene.com/cgi-bin/show.cgi?city=denver&issue=current
11. http://www.relapsedcatholic.blogspot.com/
12. http://www.guardian.co.uk/weblog/
13. http://www.spikereport.com/
14. http://slate.msn.com/code/TodaysPapers/TodaysPapers.asp
15. http://find.slate.msn.com/code/Archive/Archive.asp?Action=DepartmentSrch&GroupBy=Department&QueryText=Omnivore
16. http://www.sfbg.com/SFLife/sfblog/index.html
17. http://www.csmonitor.com/
18. http://portal.eatonweb.com
19. http://dir.yahoo.com/Social_Science/Communications/Writing/Journals_and_Diaries/Online_Journals_and_Diaries/Web_Logs/
20. http://www.userland.com/mostReadSites
21. http://www.slashdot.org/
22. http://www.kuro5hin.org/
23. http://www.freerepublic.com/
24. http://siliconvalley.com/dangillmor
25. http://doc.weblogs.com/
26. http://www.cluetrain.com/
27. http://www.amazon.com/exec/obidos/ASIN/0738204315/o/qid=991008501/sr=2-1/ref=aps_sr_b_1_1/107-5934880-4139752
28. http://doc.weblogs.com/2001/04/19
29. http://scriptingnews.userland.com/backissues/2001/05/12
30. http://davenet.userland.com/2001/05/14/deathAndDouglasAdams
31. http://www.scripting.com/
32. http://www.scripting.com/

33. http://davenet.userland.com/2001/04/24/amateursAndProse
34. http://davenet.userland.com/2001/04/17/theWebIsAWritingEnvironment
35. http://glennf.com/blog/2001/04/19.html
36. http://buzz.weblogs.com/2001/04/18
37. http://doc.weblogs.com/2001/04/19
38. http://web.siliconvalley.com/content/sv/2001/04/22/opinion/dgillmor/weblog/
index.htm

Chapter 31

1. http://www.contenu.nu/nublog.html
2. http://www.metascene.net/weblog.html
3. http://www.drmenlo.com/home.html
4. http://www.andrewsullivan.com/
5. http://web.siliconvalley.com/content/sv/opinion/dgillmor/weblog/
6. http://www.poynter.org/medianews/
7. http://www.contenu.nu/article.htm?id=1144
8. http://www.contenu.nu/article.htm?id=1145

Chapter 32

1. http://www.sunspot.net/entertainment/tv/bal-to.geraldo15dec15.story?coll=
bal-artslife-tv
2. http://www.dynamist.com/
3. http://www.andrewsullivan.com/
4. http://www.blogger.com/
5. http://www.kausfiles.com/
6. http://www.nationalreview.com/goldberg/goldberg011102.shtml
7. http://www.upi.com/view.cfm?StoryID=28122001–050733–7164r
8. http://www.instapundit.com/
9. http://www.guardian.co.uk/Archive/Article/0,4273,4260486,00.html
10. http://www.kenlayne.com/
11. http://www.mattwelch.com/warblog.html
12. http://www.buzzmachine.com/
13. http://bearstrong.net/warblog/index.html
14. http://www.blogorama.com/
15. http://blogsofwar.blogspot.com/
16. http://www.littlegreenfootballs.com/weblog/weblog.php
17. http://www.moonfarmer.org/war/
18. http://history.acusd.edu/gen/WW2Timeline/Taylorthesis.html
19. http://readjacobs.com/quickreads/jan2002_quickreads.htm
20. http://kenlayne.com/2000/2002_01_06_logarc.html
21. http://us.imdb.com/Title?0144969
22. http://www.rebeccablood.net/essays/weblog_history.html
23. http://www.suck.com/
24. http://www.links.net/
25. http://www.netsurf.com/nsd/
26. http://coursesa.matrix.msu.edu/~hst306/documents/indust.html
27. http://instapundit.blogspot.com/
28. http://www.dynamist.com/scene.html

29. http://www.dynamist.com/scene/feb12.html
30. http://www.opinionjournal.com/best/?id=95001725
31. http://www.muslimpundit.com/
32. http://blogsofwar.blogspot.com/
33. http://www.littlegreenfootballs.com/weblog/?entry=2170
34. http://bearstrong.net/warblog/index.html
35. http://sfgate.com/cgi-bin/article.cgi?f=/n/a/2002/01/15/international0640EST0497.DTL&nl=fix
36. http://sfgate.com/columnists/morford/archive/
37. http://www.observer.com/pages/story.asp?ID=5326
38. http://www.moonfarmer.org/war/
39. http://blowback.blogspot.com/?/2002_01_01_blowback_archive.html
40. http://damianpenny.blogspot.com/
41. http://quantrill.tripod.com/MCJ.html
42. http://www.buzzmachine.com/
43. http://s1.amazon.com/exec/varzea/subst/fx/help/how-we-know.html/103–3711878–0818269
44. http://nataliesolent.blogspot.com/
45. http://kenlayne.com/2000/2001_10_14_logarc.html
46. http://mattwelch.com/old/2001_10_14_archive.html
47. http://www.commondreams.org/views01/1014–01.htm
48. http://www.kathyshaidle.com/cgi-bin/itsmy/go.exe?page=6&domain=1&webdir=kathyshaidle
49. http://www.sfgate.com/cgi-bin/article.cgi?file=/chronicle/archive/2001/12/23/ED68324.DTL
50. http://quantrill.tripod.com/MCJ.html
51. http://www.lileks.com/screed/salter2.html
52. http://denbeste.nu/entries/00001675.shtml
53. http://www.readjacobs.com/quickreads/dec_quickreads.htm
54. http://instapundit.blogspot.com/?/2001_12_23_instapundit_archive.html
55. http://denbeste.nu/cd_log_entries/2002/01/fog0000000144.shtml
56. http://charlesmurtaugh.blogspot.com/?/2001_11_25_charlesmurtaugh_archive.html
57. http://timblair.blogspot.com/

Chapter 33

1. http://www.metafilter.com/
2. Matthew22:39- "And a second is like it, You shall love your neighbor as yourself."
3. http://www.digital-web.com /features/feature_2001–8.shtml

Chapter 34

1. http://metatalk.metafilter.com/mefi/1614
2. http://www.metafilter.com/mefi/13810
3. http://metatalk.metafilter.com/mefi/1647
4. http://freespace.virgin.net/matthew.champion/buttonmoon.htm
5. http://www.spork.org/
6. http://www.goaskalice.columbia.edu/1292.html

Glossary

The following list, far from being exhaustive, should be used as an introductory guide to some of the lexicon commonly used in the articles in this anthology and on weblogs in general. Due to their inclusion in this anthology, I've included some of the more popular programs and sites for the development of blogs. For a more complete list, I suggest visiting Weblog Madness's Roll Your Own page (http://www.larkfarm.com/wlm/roll_your_own.htm).

404   1. (n) A bad or broken link. Short for 404 Page Not Found. 2. (n) An HTTP status code that indicates the page requested cannot be found. Due to the nature of the Web, URLs often disappear or change. When a nonexistent page is requested, it results in the 404 page appearing. For more information, go to http://www.plinko.net/404.

The A-list   (n) The group of webloggers other bloggers deem as the best. Originally referred to the staff of Pyra and other weblog pioneers, but has come to mean any weblogger who is generally regarded by his or her peers as a celebrity in the blogging world. Can and is often used sarcastically to connote a blogger whose ego has gotten the best of him. Coined by Joe Clark in a response to Rebecca Mead's article, "You've Got Blog."

Blog, Blogging   1. (n) A shortened form of weblog. Derived from Dave Winer's pronunciation of weblog as wee-blog. 2. (v) to enter link and content into a weblog. See Blogger.

Blogdex   (n) A site developed by MIT media laboratories to track the appearance of memes in the blogging community. Located at http://blogdex.media.mit.edu. See Meme.

Blogger   1. (n) A source of code to create and maintain weblogs, developed by Pyra and distributed free of cost. Blogger provides templates and code to users who sign up and allows them to create their own weblogs without needing to know HTML or any other code. 2. (n) One who blogs.

Blogger Pro   (n) A subscription-based version of Blogger for companies and groups to use. Introduced in 2002, Blogger Pro is a modified version of Blogger that is geared toward meeting businesses' online weblogging needs. *See* Blogger, Blog.

Blognose, Blognosing   (v) To kiss up to others on your weblog. Variant based on brown-nosing.

Blogorrhea   (n) The tendency of bloggers to begin posting the minutiae of their life in an effort to keep their weblog active.

Blogroll, Blogrolling   (v) Linking or listing other weblogs that you enjoy or have some meaning to you. Coined by Doc Searles.

Blogspeak   (n) Terminology and language specific to weblogs and bloggers.

Bookmarks   (n) Links to webpages saved by the user to special folders on their browsers. Also called favorites.

Cam   (n) Shortened form of webcam. *See* Webcam.

Celeblogs   (n) Weblogs maintained by celebrities. *See* http://www.wilwheaton.net or http://www.curry.com or http://www.joe rogan.net

Cluetrain, Cluetrain Manifesto   (n) The 95 theses presented on the Cluetrain website (http://www.cluetrain.com) to help businesses understand that the Web was, more than anything else, a conversation rather than a selling tool. Authored by Rick Levine, Christopher Locke, Doc Searles, and David Weinberger.

Chat room   (n) Place where groups of people with similar interests can get together and chat in real time. Most chat rooms are offered by specific ISPs and do not always need special programs (IRCs, see below). Chat rooms have become the meeting places of the Web. *See* Instant Message, ICQ, IRC.

Community weblog   (n) A weblog built to allow more than one person to post. Often community weblogs will have a few moderators who oversee posting and comments, and several registered users who regularly post and discuss front page links. A few examples are http://www.meta filter.com, http://www.evolt.com, http://www.kuro5hin.org, and http://www.fark.com.

Daypop Top 40   (n) Site that tracks the frequency of memes in the blogging community and lists the top 40 most linked pages on weblogs. Also has a search function. Can be found at http://www.daypop.com/top.htm. *See* Meme, Blogdex.

Diaryland   (n) Created in 1999 by Andrew Smales as a site for on-line diaries. All weblogs or diaries on Diaryland stay within the domain. Unlike Blogger or Greymatter, you cannot keep your blog on your server.

Editthispage   (n) The previous name for Userland's Manilasites, software that helped create online weblogs. A button on manila site that would allow authorized users to add or change the page. *See* Manila.

Ego-surf, Ego-surfing   (v) The practice of using search engines to look for references to your name or your company's name on webpages and Web documents. Originally appeared in Gareth Branwyn's Jargon Watch column in *Wired* magazine.

FAQ (Frequently Asked Questions)   (n) A sheet or page developed by the website's owner or developer to answer the most asked questions. FAQs are attempts by the site to cut down on the amount of email sent by new users.

Flame, Flaming, Flamer   (n) A post or comment in which one person viciously attacks another's comments or posts. Sometimes personal and usually very insulting, a flame is designed to shame the other poster into silence. *See* Flamebait, Troll.

Flamebait   (n) A link, comment, or post purposefully written to create a strong reaction from other posters. The goal behind flamebait is to start a flamewar on the discussion. *See* Flame, Troll.

Fleshmeet   (n) A live person-to-person meeting. Used especially for people who only know each other through their online presence. *See* Meatspace.

Fram   (n) Spam from friends. Emails of jokes, lists, websites, and interesting tidbits with huge distribution lists that are often forwarded and in turn forwarded to others. *See* Spam.

Greymatter   (n) PERL-based server application that allows you to create any kind of weblog you want. Instead of using others' templates and server space, Greymatter allows you to develop your own look and feel.

Hacker, H4X0R　1.(n) A clever programmer. 2. (n) Someone who tries to break into other computers. A hacker for the most part means someone who really knows the systems they are working on. Unfortunately, the media has used this interchangeably with a cracker, who is someone who uses their knowledge of systems for destructive purposes.

HTML, Hypertext Markup Language　(n) A programming language or code that marks up text in order to define the look of that text on a webpage.

ICQ (I seek you)　(n) A free program that alerts you to when other users are online and allows you to contact them. Similar to Instant Messaging, ICQ allows users to chat, but it also allows users to page each other, participate in direct calls from computer to computer, play multi-player games, and send files, URLs, and emails. *See* Instant Message, IRC, Chat room.

Instant Message, Instant Messaging, IM　(n) Programs that allow users to locate others online and chat in real time over the computer. Similar in concept to chat rooms, but allows for one-to-one interface. Every major ISP now offers some kind of IM program—AIM (AOL Instant Messaging), MSNIM (Microsoft Network Instant Message), Jabber (an open-source IM), and Yahoo's Instant Messaging are four of the more popular services.

IP address　(n) A 32-bit number that identifies each sender and receiver of a packet of information across a network or the World Wide Web.

IRC (Internet Relay Chat)　(n) A place where users can chat with each other on client/server software. IRC networks allow for chat rooms or channels where users can join and freely converse (as long as they adhere to the IRC's rules and conditions). More of a communal meeting, IRCs differ from IM by focusing on groups of people, whereas IM is generally done by two parties who know each other. *See* Instant Message, ICQ, Chat rooms.

ISP (Internet Service Provider)　(n) A company that provides individuals or companies access to the Web and help in using the Internet, email, and other online programs.

l33t, 1337　(adj) Hacker-speak for elite. One of the best. Someone who has proven themselves. One of the few words in hackerspeak to be used by a wide audience.

Hyperlink   (n) An HTML-coded tag to another webpage or weblog. A hyperlink is the primary connector between sites on the Web.

Linkslut   1. (n) A website owner who loves to be linked by other webpages. 2. (n) A website owner who often links to several other sites or blogs in their commentary in hopes of receiving a link back.

Livejournal   (n) An online free service that allows you to keep a journal on their space. Similar to Diaryland and Pitas. Livejournal is an open source project with the philosophy that all the users help to create and improve the site. Currently, a new user needs a referral from a Livejournal member to start an account.

Lurk, Lurkers   (v) To read pages without commenting or posting. A lurker visits a page or blog without adding anything to the page. Most online communities encourage newbies to lurk for awhile until they get a better understanding of the site. *See* Trolling, Flame.

Manila   (n) An online publishing program. It is a server application that allows you to create and maintain websites through easy-to-use interfaces. As of October 2001, Manila was no longer offering free trials.

Meatspace   (n) The physical world. *See* Fleshmeet.

MetaFilter, MeFi   (n) A community weblog created and maintained by Matt Haughey. Allows members to post a link on a front page to webpages with a brief description. Another link below goes to a commentary section where other members can discuss the link. Often shortened to MeFi, which can also refer to a registered user on MetaFilter. *See* Community weblog.

Meme   (n) A rapidly spreading cultural idea that will commonly reappear in various aspects of a culture. Originally devised by scientist Richard Dawkins as a unit of cultural meaning on the Web, it has come to mean any website, quiz, game, or rant that is linked or sent to friends often enough that it gains a noticeable notoriety. Go to http://www.memepool.com or http://blogdex.media.mit.edu for examples.

Microportal   (n) Another term for weblogs, especially early weblogs. A microportal connotes an individual or small group of people running a site rather than a large organization. Rarely used now.

Moveable Type   (n) A PERL-based Web publishing system that runs on a user's webserver. For more information go to http://www.moveabletype.org.

Newslog   (n) An early precursor of today's weblog. A newslog filters links from other pages and posts a rolling log of current news stories, usually with minimal commentary. Also called a filter.

Online diary   (n) Another name for Online Journals (see definition below). *See* also Weblogs.

Online journal, Journaling   (n) A daily or regular posting on the Web of a person's thoughts, opinions, and ideas. Usually light on links, a journal will more often be a reflective entry on an individual's personal life. *See* Online diary, Weblogs.

Open Source, Open Source Movement   (n) Any program whose source code is available for anyone to examine and modify. Open source software is developed with the intent of wide distribution, modification and sharing. The Open Source Movement is an attempt by programmers to collaborate on software and improve it through this collaboration. In open source there is no proprietor and the user is responsible for maintaining and developing their systems. Examples of open source software are Mozilla and Linux.

Permalink   (n) A link that refers to a specific article or comment. Common on weblogs and other sites that update daily. A permalink will lead you directly to an older article after it has been removed from the site's front page. *See* Link.

Pierre Salinger Syndrome   (n) The tendency to believe that all information posted online is true.

Pitas   (n) Probably one of the easiest to use online publishing programs. With Pitas, you choose your design and load text on it with a form. Very little knowledge of HTML is needed. Ideal for online diaries and journals.

Pop-under   (n) A website or, more commonly, a Web advertisement that opens in a new browser window hidden under the current browser window. The most infamous pop-under campaign was developed for the X10 Wireless Video Camera ads, which bought advertising rights from several large company websites. *See* Pop-up.

Pop-up   (n) A website or Web advertisement that opens in a new smaller window when you enter or exit a page, click on a link, or roll over a specific spot. Used by businesses to sell subscriptions or announce great offers. There are several programs now available to stop the pop-up from populating a user's desktop. *See* Pop-under.

Post (n) A new entry of content to a site. On weblogs posts are added in a chronological order, with the most recent ones on top. 2. (v) To add commentary, a link, or a picture on a website or a weblog. *See* Threads.

Presurfer (n) Someone who surfs the Web, culls the best links and posts them on their front page. An early term for a weblogger. Rarely used now.

Pyra Labs (n) Company founded in 1999 to build power Web tools. The staff of Pyra was Evan Williams, Meg Hourihan, Paul Bausch, Matt Hamer, Matt Haughey, Jack Saturn, and Derek Powazek. Pyra created and released Blogger in 1999. *See* Blogger.

Sexblog (n) A weblog dealing with adult and mature content.

Slashdot, /. (n) A community weblog focused on technology and computer news. Owned by OSDN Inc. (Open Source Development Network), Slashdot is also an example of an open source weblog. *See* Open Source.

South by Southwest Conference, SXSW (n) An annual conference that takes place in Austin, Texas. South by Southwest is a ten-day conference, trade show, and festival for music, film, and Internet industries. Visit their website at http://www.sxsw.com/interactive/.

Spam (n) Unsolicited advertisements sent via email.

Thread (n) A link or comment on a webpage or weblog that will lead to a discussion. *See* Post.

Tip jar (n) A system for micropayments and donations to websites. Common on journals and weblogs, tipjars are links that offer the reader a chance to donate some money to the creator of the site as a thank-you for the content. There are several sites that offer this kind of service, from Amazon's Honor System, to PayPal's tip jar, to Tipjar.com.

Troll, trolling 1. (v) To read webpages without commenting or adding content. 2. (v) To post to a discussion group an incorrect or incendiary comment in order to create responses. 3. (n) One who trolls. *See* Flame, Flamebait, Lurk.

URL (Uniform Resource Locator) (n) The address of a file or resource on the Internet. For the World Wide Web, URLs are based on the HTTP protocol and are the addresses you type in on your Internet browser.

Usenet   (n) The collection of available newsgroups on the World Wide Web. Usenet is a giant collection of posting from the birth of the Web until today on a variety of subjects.

War blog   (n) This term came into prominence after September 11, 2001. These weblogs generally focus on the escalations in the Middle East and link to stories/articles pertaining to Afghanistan, Osama bin Laden, and Operation Enduring Freedom.

Webcam   (n) Digital camera hooked up to a computer that provides either live feeds or pictures at specific intervals of the user. A shortened compound of web camera. Used by many bloggers to attach an image of themselves to their writings.

Weblog   (n) Initially a weblog (or blog for short) was a chronological listing of links that the blogger thought were interesting, funny, informative, etc, with commentary. Can now mean anything from online journals and diaries, to just links then commentary. *See* Blog, Online journal, Online diary.

Webring   (n) A group of weblogs that link to each other to form a small interconnected community. Each weblog remains separate from the others, but will often link and refer to the other weblogs in the ring.

The WELL   (n) The Whole Earth 'Lectronic Link was developed in 1985 and became one of the first online communities. It founded the Electronic Frontier Foundation and set the stage for the current Web culture. It is currently owned by the Salon Media Group and can be found at http://www.well.com.

Links

Listed below are a variety of sites that are helpful in understanding weblog culture, but for various reasons did not or could not fit in with this book. Also note that I've tried to limit the number of sites listed here as either starting places (see Weblog Madness) or sites that have become somewhat legendary with the blogging community.

Starting Points

Aaronland: Weblogs, Theory, and Practice (http://aaronland.net/weblog/theory/)
The Complete Guide to Weblogs (http://www.lights.com/weblogs/)
Weblog Madness (http://www.larkfarm.com/wlm/)

Build Your Blog

Blogger (http://www.blogger.com)
Diarist.net (http://www.diarist.net/)
Diaryland (http://www.diaryland.com)
Greymatter (http://noahgrey.com/greysoft/)
Groksoup (http://www.groksoup.com)
Livejournal (http://www.livejournal.com/)
Manila (http://www.manilasites.com/)
Moveable Type (http://www.moveabletype.org)
Open Journal (http://www.grohol.com/downloads/oj/)
Pitas (http://www.pitas.com/)

Search Engines

Dogpile (http://www.dogpile.com)
Google (http://www.google.com)
Open Directory Project (http://dmoz.org/)
Yahoo (http://www.yahoo.com)

News Sources

Alternet (http://www.alternet.org/)
Associated Press (http://wire.ap.org)
Jim Romenesko's Media News (http://www.poynter.org/medianews/)
Independent Media Center (http://www.indymedia.org/)
Infojunkie (http://www.infojunkie.com)
Obscure Store (http://www.obscurestore.com)
Online Journalism Review (http://ojr.usc.edu/)
Robot Wisdom (http://www.robotwisdom.com)
Tomalak's Realm (http://www.tomalak.org)

Meme Tracking Sites

Blogdex (http://blogdex.media.mit.edu)
Daypop (http://www.daypop.com)
Memepool (http://www.memepool.com)

Community Weblogs

Evolt (http://www.evolt.org/)
Fark (http://www.fark.com)
Geeknews (http://www.geeknews.net/)
Kuro5hin (http://www.kuro5hin.org/)
Linkfilter (http://www.linkfilter.net/)
MetaFilter (http://www.metafilter.com)
Oceanblog (http://www.davidgagne.net/oceans/)
Plastic (http://www.plastic.com)

Dictionaries, Encyclopedias, and Other Resources

Blog Dictionary (http://www.davidgagne.net/main/dictionary.shtml)
Whatis?.com (http://whatis.techtarget.com/)
Word Spy (http://www.logophilia.com/WordSpy/)

Everything Else

Behind the Curtain: A Day in the Life of Webloggers (http://www.zopesite.com/behindthecurtain/)
The Bloggies (http://www.fairvue.com/?feature=awards2002)
Blog Elements (http://www.fairvue.com/?feature=elements2)
Blogstickers (http://www.blogstickers.com)
Friday Five (http://fridayfive.org)
Weblog Junior High (http://www.wrongwaygoback.com/wjh/)
The Whyilog (http://www.stormpages.com/totalchaos/whyilog.html)

Contributors

Cameron Barrett has been working in the Web design field since 1995 after co-founding an Internet Service Provider. In 1998 he joined the team at Borders.com and designed their first website. He worked for two years at a leading open source company, taking the concepts of open source software development methodology into Fortune 100 companies. He is currently working for a firm on Wall Street developing user interfaces for financial services Web applications. He is well known for developing some of the first Mozilla browser themes and is hard at work editing several computer books for O'Reilly. He speaks regularly at Web design and development conferences and edits one of the longest running weblogs on the Internet. Visit him at CamWorld (www.camworld.com).

Rebecca Blood has been creating websites since 1996. She maintains Rebecca's Pocket (www.rebeccablood.net), a weblog focused on culture and society. Her first book, *The Weblog Handbook*, will be published in June by Perseus Publishing. She lives in San Francisco.

starvingartist (Joshua Brown) is a Cleveland actor and stage combat choreographer who surfs the Net on the side. He went to school at Case Western Reserve University, and is the Managing Director of the Cleveland Shakespeare Festival. He hopes one day to work in films.

Tim Cavanaugh is a San Francisco–based writer whose work has appeared in the *San Francisco Chronicle*, New York *Newsday*, Agence France-Presse, *San Francisco* Magazine, *Wired, Reason, Request, Salon, Feed, Mother Jones, The Manhattan Spirit*, the *Orange County Weekly* and other publications. He edited the late Suck.com and can still be attacked at Simpleton.com.

Joe Clark (joeclark@joeclark.org) is a Toronto writer who has been online since 1991, two years after he began a career as a journalist writing for magazines and newspapers. His portfolio includes 390 print articles, over 500 pages at his various websites (joeclark.org, fawny.org, contenu.nu), and the book *Building Accessible Websites* (New Riders, 2002). He maintains a personal weblog, another on online content, a third on Web accessibility, and a fourth on the book-writing process, all of them widely unread. (See joeclark.org/weblogs/.)

Snarkout (Steve Cook) thinks that mundane things are usually the most interesting of all and writes about Victorian criminals, mechanical chess players, libertines, baseball, and beer at snarkout.org. He shares his home outside Washington, D.C. with a delightful person and a magnificently irritating cat.

Julian Dibbell has been writing about digital culture for over a decade. His first book, *My Tiny Life: Crime and Punishment in a Virtual World*, was published by Henry Holt in 1998. His essays and articles have appeared in *Feed*, *Wired*, *The Village Voice*, *Harper's*, *Time*, and in numerous anthologies, including *Flame Wars* (Duke) and *Reading Digital Culture* (Blackwell). He lives in South Bend, Indiana.

GeekMan is a freelance website designer, graphic designer, and programmer living in New York City. Though he still believes being a graphic designer is a cool career, his mother wishes he had listened to her and gotten a 'real' job, like high school janitor or gravedigger. Apparently, he is so full of himself that he created a personal website at www.themightygeek.com, where he maintains his blog. He honestly believes that other people will find it entertaining, and even though he is proven wrong on a daily basis, he continues to write in the hopes of one day taking over the world. No one takes him seriously, not even himself.

Glenn Fleishman is a freelance journalist in Seattle who contributes to the *New York Times*, the *Seattle Times*, *Fortune Magazine*, *Wired Magazine*, *O'Reilly Networks*, and other publications. He formerly ran one of the first Web development firms, founded in 1994, and worked for six months at Amazon.com. His two weblogs, one personal/professional and the other in wireless networking, were read by over 1,000 visitors daily near the end of 2001.

Brad Graham is an author, editor, raconteur, bon vivant, freelance factotum, and singer of sentimental ballads. His writing has appeared in publications around the country, mostly in the form of bitterly worded personal ads. A native of Missouri, he is proud to live and work in St. Louis, the Gateway to the Rectangular States.

Matt Haughey has been building websites since 1995 and weblogging since 1999. He built MetaFilter.com to learn a new programming language, and ended up with a bustling community of over 13,000 members. The site has been mentioned in major newspapers worldwide, various Internet magazines, and appeared on CNN and TechTV. Matthew was recently named one of the "top 25 Web personalities" by *Shift Magazine* and is currently writing a new book about weblogs and working as a freelance developer in San Francisco.

Jon Katz is a columnist for Slashdot and author of *Geeks: How Two Lost Boys Rode the Internet out of Idaho.*

J. D. Lasica is a senior columnist with the *Online Journalism Review* (http://ojr.usc.edu) and a former editorial manager at three new media startups. In a prior life he spent 11 years as an editor and columnist with the *Sacramento Bee.* He lives in the San Francisco Bay Area with his wife and young son.

Marquis (Sean Michaels) is a writer of stories. He is co-editor of TANG-MONKEY.COM (http://www.tangmonkey.com).

Rebecca Mead has been a staff writer at the *New Yorker* since 1997. Before that, she was a contributing editor at *New York* magazine and a writer for the *Sunday Times* of London. She received her B.A. from Oxford University and her M.A. from New York University.

Nikolai Nolan's presence on the Web began in 1997 with a site on GeoCities that he would like to forget. His first notable site was Splitzy's Planet of the Space Monkeys (www.spacemonkeys.net), the largest site in existence about the cartoon "Captain Simian and the Space Monkeys." He continued on to create his award-winning personal site, Fairvue Central (www.fairvue.com). Fairvue includes a weblog and numerous features such as Blog.Elements (the Periodic Table of Weblogs), the Voice Mail Megamix, and the Blog Song. Each year Nikolai holds the Weblog Awards (also known as the "Bloggies") which award the best weblogs of the year in many unique categories. He currently attends the University of Michigan. All this information and more can be found on his site. Check it out.

Derek Powazek is author, Web designer, community consultant, and professional troublemaker. As Powazek Productions (powazek.com), he created community-rich sites like (fray) (fray.com), Kvetch! (kvetch.com), and San Francisco Stories (sfstories.com), consulted on community features for clients like Netscape, Lotus, and Sony. His book on the design of community spaces online, *Design for Community* (designforcommunity.com), was published last year by New Riders. Derek believes in a passionate, personal Web.

Jordan Raphael is a freelance journalist based in Los Angeles. He has written for a number of publications, including the *New York Times*, the *Los Angeles Times, Inside Magazine,* and the *Online Journalism Review,* where his article originally appeared. He is currently co-writing a biography of Marvel Comics publisher Stan Lee and completing his doctoral dissertation in communication at the University of Southern California.

Rich Robinson has been online in some form since the mid-1980s and on the Web since 1995. He runs a personal website (don't call it a weblog), inferiority.com, for your pleasure and has been published online at A List Apart, the definitive site for people who make websites.

Douglas Rushkoff is author of eight books about media, technology, and culture, translated into 17 languages so far. They include *Coercion, Media Virus, Playing the Future,* and *Cyberia.* His interactive novel, *Exit Strategy,* is online now, and will be published in summer 2002. His novel *Ecstasy Club* is being made into a motion picture. Rushkoff is a Markle Foundation fellow and on the board of the Media Ecology Association. He is currently working on a new book about "Open Source Judaism" called *Nothing Sacred,* teaching at New York University, and delivering commentaries on National Public Radio.

Mike Skallas is a freelance computer consulant, native Chicagoan, and self-described "sexy beast." He currently studies film at Columbia College in Chicago.

Walrus (Dan Symond) is 29 years old, male and lives in London where he works in software design. Dan has been using the Web since about 1996 and enjoys it most as a medium for publishing and collaborating creatively.

Neale Talbot is an Australian writer, poet, and super-secret double-agent. Having spent the last three years weblogging, he is, naturally, a very, very bitter man. His hobbies include fighting hypocrisy, tweaking the nipples of pretentiousness, and begging publishers for a book deal.

Tomalak's Realm started in November 1998 links to interesting articles about the Web daily. Lawrence Lee is the Editor of *Tomalak's Realm* and is based in West Vancouver, Canada.

Giles Turnbull is a freelance writer based in the U.K. He writes about the Internet and cyberculture, and contributes regular items to BBCi (www.bbc.co.uk) and WriteTheWeb (www.writetheweb.com). He has a professional home page at www.gorjuss.com, and a more relaxed personal one at www.gilest.org.

KV (Kate Vaughn) is a 24-year-old writer from Melbourne, Australia and test-drives fiction and non-fiction on papermilk.com and sincerity-bird.com.

Ron Yeany is a Web designer-developer-educator for a major Boston-area university. He's been designing and developing websites since 1994. His first site, for Penn State's student newspaper, was runner-up in *Wired Magazine's* "Best of the Web" for college newspaper sites in 1996. He has been maintaining a blog at www.leatheregg.com since March 2000.

Credits

Anatomy of a Weblog originally appeared on January 26, 1999 at Cam-World. It can be found at http://www.camworld.com/journal/rants/99/01/26.html. Copyright © 1999 by Cameron Barrett. Used by permission of the author.

Been Blogging? Web Discourse Hits Higher Level originally appeared on April 1, 2001 in the *Seattle Times* and can be found at http://archives.seattle times.nwsource.com/cgibin/texis.cgi/web/vortex/display?slug=ptblog01&dat e=20010401. Copyright © 2001 by Glenn Fleishman. Used by permission of the author.

Blogged Down in the PR Machine originally appeared on May 16, 2001 at the *Online Journalism Review*. It can be found online at http://ojr.usc.edu/content/story.cfm?request=581. Copyright © 2001 by Jordan Raphael. Used with permission of the author.

The Blogger Code originally appeared on January 9, 2002 at Leatheregg.com. It can be found online at http://www.leatheregg.com/bloggercode/. Copyright © 2002 by Ron Yeany. Used with permission of the author.

Blogging as a Form of Journalism originally appeared on May 24, 2001 in the *Online Journalism Review*. It can be found at http://ojr.usc.edu/content/story.cfm?request=585. Copyright © 2001 by J. D. Lasica. Used by permission of the author.

Blogma 2001 Missive One: Uphold the Weblog originally appeared on November 14, 2000. It can be found at http://grudnuk.com/blogma2001/. Copyright © 2000 by Blogma2001 Committee. Used by permission of the author.

Blogma 2001 Missive Two: Further Matters; and Some Clarifications originally appeared on November 18, 2000. It can be found at http://

Let Slip the Blogs of War originally appeared on January 17, 2002 at the *Online Journalism Review* website. It can be found at http://ojr.usc.edu/content/story.cfm?request=683. Copyright © 2002 by Tim Cavanaugh. Used by permission of the author.

The Libera Manifesto originally appeared on March 16, 2001 at Lockergnome.com. It can be found at http://www.lockergnome.com/manifesto.html. Copyright © 2001 by Chris Pirillo. Used by permission of the author.

Linking 1–2–3 originally appeared on December 7, 1998 at *Tomalak's Realm* and can be found online at http://www.tomalak.org/random/98/981207.html. Copyright © 1998 by Lawrence Lee. Used by permission of the author.

More About Weblogs originally appeared on May 11, 1999 at CamWorld. It can be found at http://www.camworld.com/journal/rants/99/05/11.html. Copyright © 1999 by Cameron Barrett. Used by permission of the author.

Portrait of the Blogger as a Young Man originally appeared as an Idee Fixe column in *Feed Magazine*. Copyright © 2001 by Julian Dibbell. Used by permission of the author.

Put the Keyboard Down and Back Away from the Weblog originally appeared on March 28, 2000 at *Article One*, part of www.wrongwaygoback.com. It can be found at http://www.wrongwaygoback.com/articleone/putthekeyboarddownandbackawayfromtheweblog.shtml. Copyright 2000 © by Neale Talbot. Used by permission of the author.

Ten Tips for Building a Bionic Weblog originally appeared on Metascene. It can be found at http://members.tripod.com/amused_2/bionic.html. Copyright © 2000 by Fred Pyen. Used by permission of the author.

The State of the Blog Part 1: Blogger Past originally appeared on February 26, 2001 on *WritetheWeb* and can be found online at http://writetheweb.com/read.php?item=106. Copyright © 2000 by Giles Turnbull. Used by permission of the author.

The State of the Blog Part 2: Blogger Present originally appeared on February 28, 2001 on *WritetheWeb* and can be found online at http://writetheweb.com/read.php?item=107. Copyright © 2000 by Giles Turnbull. Used by permission of the author.

The State of the Blog Part 3: Blogger Future originally appeared on March 2, 2001 on *WritetheWeb* and can be found online at http://write

theweb.com/read.php?item=108. Copyright © 2000 by Giles Turnbull. Used by permission of the author.

Weblogs: A History and Perspective originally appeared on September 7, 2000 at *What's In Rebecca's Pocket*. It can be found at http://www.rebecca blood.net/essays/weblog_history.html. Copyright © 2000 by Rebecca Blood. Used by permission of the author.

Weblogs: A New Source of News originally appeared on May 31, 2001 in the *Online Journalism Review*. It can be found at http://ojr.usc.edu/content/story.cfm?request=588. Copyright © 2001 by J. D. Lasica. Used by permission of the author.

Weblogging: Lessons Learned was originally published at Kulesh.org and can be found online at http://kulesh.org/weblog/jottings/lessons.htm. Copyright © 1999 by Kulesh Shanmugasundaram. Used by permission of the author.

Weblogs (Good God Y'all) What Are they Good For (Absolutely Nothing—Say It Again) originally appeared in Volume 1 Edition 2 *of Wrongwaygoback: fantastical* and can be found at http://www.wrongwaygoback.com/fantastical/index.asp?l=40&r=41. Copyright © 2001 by Neale Talbot. Used with permission of the author.

We Didn't Start the Weblogs originally appeared at fairvue.com and can be found online at http://www.fairvue.com/?feature=start. Copyright © 2001 by Nikolai Nolan. Used by permission of the author.

What the Hell Is a Weblog and Why Won't They Leave Me Alone? originally appeared on February 17, 2000 at Powazek Productions and can be found at http://www.powazek.com/wtf/. Copyright © 2000 by Derek Powazek. Used with permission of the author.

Why I Weblog originally appeared on June 16, 1999 at The BradLands and can be found online at http://www.bradlands.com/words/maybe/maybe02.html. Copyright © 1999 by Brad Graham. Used by permission of the author.

You've Got Blog originally appeared on November 13, 2000 in the *New Yorker* and can be found online at http://www.rebeccamead.com/2000_11_13_art_blog.htm. Copyright © 2000 by Rebecca Mead. Used by permission of the author.